# On Hinduism

# On Hinduism

## Irina Gajjar

Axios Press
PO Box 457
Edinburg, VA 22824
888.542.9467    info@axiosinstitute.org

**Library of Congress Cataloging-in-Publication Data**

    Gajjar, Irina N.
    On hinduism / Irina Gajjar.
    pages cm
    ISBN 978-1-60419-072-4 (pbk.)
    1. Hinduism. I. Title.

    BL1202.G35 2013

    294.5--dc23

                                           2013000177

# Contents

# Author's Preface

## Thanks to Readers and a Word about Authorities

Thanks to you, the reader, for your interest in this work. If you go on, you will read a book about Hinduism. You might have opened it because you are curious about Hinduism, or seriously interested in Hinduism, or find Hinduism confusing, or implausible or because you are a Hindu and wonder what to say when someone questions you about your belief. You might be a student, or a teacher. You might be a scientist, attracted by the skeptic's perspective and wondering how so many people can believe the nonsense that you think Hinduism represents. You might be a scholar and wonder how anyone can dare to present herself as an authority in a book with no references. You might be seeking a companion to *The*

*Gita, A New Translation of Hindu Sacred Scripture* published a few years ago. Whatever your viewpoint or reason for reading at least this far, I hope not to disappoint you. This book was written for you.

You do not have to read *On Hinduism* in its entirety to benefit from it. You can pick and choose among the chapters because each chapter has a different theme and each one is self-contained. If you do read the whole book, you will find some subjects revisited in different contexts and you will gain more understanding. To assist you, we have provided a complete index and glossary. To make reading convenient, I have incorporated details that could have been relegated to footnotes into the text itself. Similarly, I have explained some important terms as they appear.

Hinduism is a big subject with many facets and much as I have tried to avoid complexity, I may not have always succeeded. In some cases, I chose completeness and accuracy over simplicity. Thus, it is fine for readers to skip portions that may not address questions of immediate interest. This work is designed to be used as a reference, and readers can always revisit what was missed the first time around.

Hindu Philosophy is a dominant force in our world, as it has been for millennia. Although Hinduism is a viewpoint, like all philosophies and religions, this particular viewpoint has had great impact on large numbers of people for many thousands of years and in the twenty-first century it is marching full steam ahead. Thus, Hinduism should not be an enigma to so many.

In a sense, *On Hinduism* is an opinion about an opinion. Religions are beliefs and opinions about the universe, about humankind, about birth and death and matters of the spirit. Hinduism itself is a widely held belief system and this work is a true account of what Hindus believe. It is grounded in too many sources to list, sources that do not lend themselves to a bibliography as many details have been absorbed, shaped, and evolved as they worked themselves into this book.

The authorities upon which this work is gratefully based can be placed in four categories as follows:

## Writings

- ❖ Scripture
- ❖ Translations and commentaries on scripture
- ❖ Mythology
- ❖ Historical texts
- ❖ Biographical texts
- ❖ Philosophical texts
- ❖ Sanskrit grammars
- ❖ Annotated illustrations and photographs
- ❖ Scientific works
- ❖ Articles

◈ Dictionaries
◈ Fiction

## Word of Mouth

◈ Lectures
◈ Countless conversations in several languages with three generations of Hindu priests, philosophers, devotees, relatives, friends of Hinduism.
◈ Countless conversations in several languages with three generations of agnostics, atheists, critics of Hinduism and believers in other religions.

## Experience

◈ Participation in Hindu life over many years
◈ Participation in Hindu rituals over many years.
◈ Travel throughout the world.

## The Internet

◈ With particular appreciation for Wikipedia and many individuals and organizations who have shared their viewpoints and wisdom on many websites.

Once again, thank you for giving this book your consideration.

—Irina Gajjar

# A Skeptic's Perspective

This book is a discussion from the perspective of a scholar and believer. This commentary, however, is a discussion by a skeptic and atheist. *On Hinduism* is a comprehensive account of contemporary Hinduism: a religion that for many justifies place and existence. Yet, in discussing God and truths, there is much work to be done before our species reaches consensus.

Assumptions are the bedrock of all philosophies and their associated ideologies, world-views and paradigms. The value we attribute to such assumptions and their relevance to truth is the subject of this commentary.

Hindus addressing God and the soul assume their reality and permanence. The atheist assumes perception, experience and the existence of self to be dictated by the physical world alone. And by coupling theory with experiment, science assumes reality to be measurable. As perception is an act of measurement, the assumptions of the atheist and scientist are equivalent. For the two, discussion of the unmeasurable (without regard to practicality) is discussion of the supernatural.

Hinduism considers God to be everything, but not limited to being only everything. God is eternity, the infinite, and the finite. He is all and more. By this extension of dominion, "God" can no longer be synonymous with "everything." He now also exists amidst the supernatural or perhaps constitutes it. Where we find the supernatural is where we find the rest of God. While we cannot reasonably dispute the existence of the supernatural, the soul—which is also regarded by Hinduism as unmeasurable and eternal—is another matter entirely.

The soul will render itself superfluous to any consistent physical description of a life form. In describing a watch, if we understand all mechanisms and principles of operation, no additional concept or idea is necessary to explain its purpose, function or state. I have faith, that I do not inhabit my body, but I am because of my body. The establishment of a unified blueprint of life by science will exile the soul and the assumption of the existence of the soul will prove itself to be invalid. Thereafter, the soul will solely serve as a potent synonym for human identity.

On the other hand, the idea of reincarnation more closely represents occurrences in the natural world.

Reincarnation may be understood as a metaphor for the clustering of matter into life and its consequent return to a banal and inorganic state. While Hinduism is able to provide metaphorical aids for understanding the physical nature of existence, we can explain scientific phenomena using well-defined terminology and convention. We must appreciate that rigor and catalog enhance the possibility of consensus and thereby curtail bias.

Religious faith attempts to bridge the divide between our aspirations for knowledge and our capacity to know. However in doing so, it often disparages established though fragile truths. Do not mistake me: the limits of scientific pursuit are real. We might ask what remains after the scientific method is exhausted. While I am content to call the remainder God, conjecture should stop there—to call it anything is daring enough.

With thoughts of mourners sweating by the flames of your pyre, the futility of being is realized. Thus, the tendency to submit to indoctrination is understandable given the considerable social benefits of organized religion and the comforting promise of the immortality of self. Nonetheless, human comfort and conviction are not acceptable measures of physical truth. An evolving consensus based on physical evidence is the best approximation of truth our species can justify.

This book provides the framework necessary to consider and understand the depth and importance of Hinduism. If you are inclined, you will no doubt find comfort and wisdom in its pages. If you are not, you may be enticed to challenge the views of a convincing and distinguished writer. I regard this work as both a historical and philosophical account grounded by the deep reflections of an important mind.

—Ravi J. Heugle

# Chapter One

# Hindus and Hinduism

Those who Trust God
are on the Road to Me
But those who do not trust God
are lost

(*Gita* 3:31)

HE QUESTION, "Who is a Hindu?" is much harder to answer than the question "What is Hinduism?"

Historians, teachers, scholars, and gurus have disagreed about Hinduism for centuries and continue to disagree. Hindus themselves agree even less about who they are and what they believe. The reason is that Hinduism, while clear and simple, is a universal faith. Hinduism has powerful tenets, but they are open to interpretation and evolving scientific truth. Respect for individual thought runs deep. Alternatives abound. Hinduism is easy to understand for Hindus, but complex or varied explanations create confusion in the minds of those who have not absorbed or been absorbed by Hinduism. Numerous and divergent ideas, images, and theories confuse strangers to Hinduism while Hindus themselves find giving answers to outsiders difficult because they never considered the questions.

To believers or followers of Hinduism, their religion is a premise, a starting point, rather than a conclusion or ending point. Hinduism can be viewed as a springboard. Hindus jump off that springboard and make leaps of faith. This is why describing a Hindu as a believer in Hinduism is accurate, but at the same time incomplete and redundant. It must be true that no Hindu believes everything that has been preached in the name of Hinduism. The majority of Hindus have not even read the *Bhagavad Gita* or the *Gita* in its entirety, which is a pity as this short quintessential scripture that contains the distilled essence of Hinduism is one of the greatest writings ever written. Yet Hindus remain staunch and sophisticated in their affiliation. Their mindset is composed of philosophy, spirituality, and ethics, all colored by ritual, mythology, and tradition.

Hinduism came to India from Northwest Asia in about 1500 BCE. It arrived with Aryan (Indo-Iranian) horsemen who moved down the Indian peninsula and, by at least 500 BCE, firmly established the ancient Vedic culture that they brought with them. These newcomers overwhelmed the existing highly developed Indus Valley Civilization, already in a state of decline. The Aryans brought along little in the way of materialism, but a wealth of ancient wisdom. Their legacy comes from the *Vedas*, a body of literary scripture. The *Vedas* were originally passed down by word of mouth from generation to generation before they were recorded in Sanskrit, a rich complex language. Sanskrit gave rise to the vernacular languages of Northern India and it lives on in religious writings. At the same time, elements of the earlier Indus Valley beliefs and customs also survive in twenty-first century Hinduism.

A short definition of Hinduism may be: "A religious belief that aims at merging the soul into God." This definition acknowledges the concepts of religion, soul, and God and implies some vaguely common opinion about what these concepts represent. A longer definition may say: "Hinduism is a religion that seeks merger of the soul into God by means of loving worship, of knowledge, or of good deeds. Hindu belief is premised on a belief in karma which in turn is based on the idea of reincarnation." Most Hindus find reincarnation and karma fairly easy to understand, but they are not of one mind regarding how reincarnation works or how to worship, or what deeds are good. Nor do Hindus agree on the significance or even the existence of God.

Hinduism allows for everyone to follow an inner guide. Knowledge, faith, skepticism, agnosticism, questions, and traditions are personal and variable. Hindus may choose to follow the teachings of their family or of a guru or they may just go with the flow.

One of the vows in Hindu marriage ceremonies illustrates the importance of freedom of personal belief. Both the bride and the bridegroom encourage one another to develop their personal faith through worship that is free from interference.

The *Gita* crystallizes Hindu thought but it too is subject to interpretation. It does not require a Hindu to believe anything in particular. Instead, it glorifies goodness and truth and makes references to beliefs that are taken for granted. It addresses human doubts, questions, and fears and inspires physical and spiritual courage. This teaching illustrates the meaning of *merging into God, soul, worship, knowledge, good deeds, karma*, and *reincarnation*. It sets forth diverse and sometimes opposing criteria for attaining enlightenment or becoming one with the infinite which, according to Hindu theory, represents ultimate bliss.

God is implicit, though debated in Hinduism. He is an idea that cannot be grasped by the human mind, a presumption regarding an absolute, awesome eternal energy worthy of adoration.

God is separate and distinct from the gods of mythology who romp about as did the gods in Greek and Roman myths. God is also separate from His human incarnations. Both in myths and in scripture, Divine Avatars act on behalf of God's invisible, unfathomable form. Lord Krishna, an Avatar of Lord Vishnu, the Preserver, who is believed to be the source of all other Avatars, explains:

> I am born from time to time
> whenever the good need my protection.
> I am born to destroy the bad and help the
> good.

(*Gita* 4:7)

The Hindu Divinity is the flame of truth envisioned by humans to be in harmony with the light that shines within. Because individual perceptions of the absolute differ greatly from one another, Hindu philosophy seamlessly conjoins and separates symbols, ideas, stories, and beliefs that pertain to God or to gods. As God is the Creator, the Destroyer, the Preserver as well as invisible, omnipresent, omnipotent, indestructible, and one with us, there is no perception that any divine representation or symbolism whatsoever could be flawed.

While Hinduism understands that God is beyond the grasp of human thought, it also acknowledges God's tremendous power over our human minds and lives. As the quest for enlightenment is the quest to become one with God, Hinduism strives to bring humankind to oneness with divinity.

Hindu philosophy gives great importance to the soul or spirit which it distinguishes from the mind as well as from the body. Hinduism equates the spirit with God. Chapter thirteen of the *Bhagavad Gita* explains that the spirit cannot be described, that it cannot act, that it is always pure and endless as the sun and the sky. God is considered the greatest spirit. Thus, to Hindus, finding our soul is akin to finding infinity within us. It equates to achieving a perfection which can only be attained by a highly evolved soul, a soul that over many lifetimes has superseded the limitations of humanness.

Though Hindus know deeply that the ultimate aim of their faith is to achieve unity with God, daily life and worship generally focus on more immediate results. Karma may take ages to play out, but the laws of cause and effect that are its foundation may also operate more quickly. Divine intervention works hand in hand with karma that is created by human behavior. Thus, worship is a path to enlightenment and simply setting forth on this path has its own validity. Progressing on the path to God is not only about reaching a destination. Making the journey earns merit in itself.

Hindu scriptures and customs consider a wide range of activities as worship: fulfillment of duty, prayer, pursuit of knowledge, honoring elders and teachers, tending to shrines in the home, visiting temples, going on pilgrimages, bathing in holy waters, practicing moderation, fasting, performing rituals, chanting, engaging in meditation and yoga, attending and participating in ceremonies, listening to preachers, performing classical dance, and so on. These activities are incorporated into secular life. Though none of them are singly defining, it is virtually certain that routine customs and occurrences will engage just about every Hindu in some overt forms of worship. Mindsets may differ regarding the value or effect of these variegated activities, but participating in some of them is unavoidable.

The vast array of practices that make up worship in Hinduism may befuddle strangers to such rituals. Although most ritualistic acts and sacrifices have specific and generally known purposes, collectively their aim is to enhance the mind's focus and thereby to extend consciousness. These ceremonies as well as actions undertaken in the name of God or goodness acknowledge and revere a power higher and greater than the power of the human mind or the human heart. Whatever form worship takes, be it worship of God or of another deity, worship in any form acknowledges the existence of something greater than humankind. Chapter four of the *Gita,* "The Sword of Knowledge," explains:

A puja is a ceremony for God.
It is a sacrifice.
The puja is Brahma [God].
The fire which is part of the puja is Brahma.
The person who performs the puja is Brahma.
Brahma is God's everlasting power.
We cannot see or hear or feel Brahma.
Reaching Brahma and understanding Brahma
is the reason for the puja.

(*Gita* 4:24, 25)

These particular verses refer to ritualistic ceremonies; however, other passages recognize that anything at all done in the name of God ultimately leads to freedom and to merging oneself into the absolute being.

Although Hinduism glorifies God, it does not require its followers to accept God's power or even God's existence. Doubt may be a starting point. Hindu scripture, philosophy, and Hindus themselves believe that attaining knowledge of truth could take lifetimes. Meanwhile, following the right course provides ongoing rewards. Self-betterment can bring peace of mind as well as material improvements not only in future lifetimes, but also in the present lifetime. Prayers may be answered, even if uttered by disbelievers. The act of praying or making a sacrifice, or purposefully doing a good deed in itself implies belief in the possibility that the prayer or sacrifice or deed will invoke the intervention of a force capable of delivering results.

Hinduism defines knowledge as more than the acquisition of information. Knowledge pertains first and foremost to knowing God. This covers everything from seeking God, to knowing about God, to understanding God, or to feeling God. Chapter seven of the *Bhagavad Gita*, "Knowing God," offers a road map to the unveiling of the mystery of life. It explains that of the countless people who exist, only a few seek God and that of those few, only a handful gain a true understanding of divinity.

True knowledge pertains to understanding the Creator who causes the worlds and is the "life principle" or the essence of life. In his incarnation as Lord Krishna, God says that He is composed of earth, water, fire, air, ether, mind, reason, and the self. He tells us that He is the wetness in water, the light in the moon and sun, and the sacred symbol Om which encompasses God and the Universe:

> I am the manliness in men
> and the smell of the earth
> and the brightness in fire.
> I am life in living things.

I am the seed in all beings.
I am the wisdom in men's minds.
I am the strength of the strong
and the wish in your heart.

(*Gita* 7:9, 10, 11)

Knowledge means understanding that God is
the only reality, because only God, the absolute, is
unchanging and constant. The physical world is an illusion that creates attachment and desire which distract,
confuse, and blind us. They haze our vision, but the
quest for understanding dispels ignorance and opens
our eyes to God who is ever present for all to see.

The quest for secular knowledge is included in the
quest for wisdom aimed at knowing the absolute. All
knowledge contributes to solving the big puzzle that
motivates inquiry. Human beings cannot identify, let
alone put together, the pieces of this puzzle. We do not
know the right questions, let alone the right answers,
to questions like *How big is the Universe? Where did the
Universe start? Where does it end? What moves it? Who
are we? Where did we come from? Where are we headed
after death?* Yet, these questions pursue us. Thus,
though the ultimate truth is a mystery, truth learned
through the pursuit of knowledge is ultimate.

Hindus consider that along with worship and knowledge, the path of good action also leads to unity with
God. In a sense, the three paths become one because

deeds, worship, and seeking knowledge are actions in themselves. In chapter three of the *Bhagavad Gita,* "God Explains Right Action," Lord Krishna points out that the world and God himself cannot function without action. However, while the paths of worship, knowledge, and action all lead to God, all action does not. Only good deeds performed with detachment from their outcome do. Detachment requires surrendering the results of our deeds to a higher power. Actions taken with attachment to their fruit do not lead to anything. Doing your best and letting God do the rest is the path to enlightenment. Beyond doing your best, performing good deeds in fulfillment of duty rather than in pursuit of a specific result leads to complete knowledge of God.

Like people, actions have their own results and destinies. Results are determined by the characters of the actors that brought them about and by the characters and destinies of all the participants in the intertwined chain of events that influenced them. To understand this notion is to be able to strive without focusing on the outcome of our effort. So while it is not easy to act without being result oriented, and while the world judges by results, it is important to recognize that the results of our efforts are not always in our hands.

Naturally, the idea of detachment cannot cause people to disassociate themselves from goals. Part of doing your best requires a focus on outcome. In preparing for an exam that could determine your future, you must consider the grading system. But you can detach by understanding that factors beyond your control—like a curve or the examiner's bias—may determine how you fare. Detachment facilitates concentration. Letting the chips fall where they may leaves the outcome of your efforts to chance or God and frees you from attachment.

Hindu philosophy considers that karma predicts and determines the consequences of all actions. Karma does not quite equate to destiny. Predetermination forges destiny, whereas karma generates and regenerates itself when beings act. Karma incorporates the law of cause and effect that says what goes around comes around. It also reflects the laws of physics that say energy is not lost or created. Karma is relative in that it is not restricted by time or by space, at least not in the sense that human beings understand these limitations. In other words, karma is not necessarily confined to our planet or our lifetime. Although it may work quickly, it creates itself and plays itself out in any time frame and in any or many spaces within the universe or universes. Karma goes on and on until the authors of the actions that trigger it merge into the supreme being or perhaps cease to exist. At such a time they and their karma become part of the cosmic energy pool.

Different Hindus perceive the relationship between God and karma in different ways. Some go so far as to say that karma determines the future and God does not exist or matter at all. Some equate the divine force with karma or believe that God creates karma and hence see no issue regarding interaction between the two. Yet other individuals and Hindu schools of thought, more conventionally, see God as the dispenser of karma, which He possibly tempers with divine mercy. Whatever their particular viewpoint, Hindu philosophers and laymen agree with the viewpoint that good behavior earns merit and improves their karma and that misfortune is the product of prior bad behavior. Even those who do not fully believe in karmic power generally consider the idea of karma a plausible guideline for ethical living.

The concept of karma complements the theory of reincarnation. Since karma does not play out in the context of one lifetime, actions performed in earlier lifetimes account for reactions that occur in later ones. Reincarnation means rebirth in the flesh, or re-embodiment. Most Hindus believe in reincarnation. The idea that human beings have been born and died before is pivotal in the *Gita* and other religious and philosophical texts. Lord Krishna explains this to Arjun, India's great epic hero, on the brink of battle:

> Oh, Arjun, birth leads to death and death
>     leads to birth,
> so do not grieve over something that cannot
>     be helped
> Everyone died before he was born
> and was born before he died.
> So what is there to be sad about?
> All creatures are formless before birth
> and formless after death.
> They only have form during life
> which is between birth and death.
>
> (*Gita* 2:26, 27, 28)

Although reincarnation is not confined to earth, human experience and memory often limit ideas of birth and rebirth to our world. Most references to other worlds and beings come from myths that tantalize minds with vivid details empowering Hindus to see their belief in colorful dimensions. Philosophy and mythology incorporate karma and reincarnation suggesting that something lies between earthly existence and unity with the absolute or unity with nothingness.

Hinduism sets forth a comprehensive world view. However, the breadth, depth, and boundlessness of this view may perplex those unaccustomed to following alternative trains of thought. For example, though Hindus take God's multiple roles of Creator, Preserver, and Destroyer for granted, others may consider these roles in conflict, failing to take into account that they represent the cycles followed by the universe.

Similarly, non-Hindus may consider worshiping an absolute God incongruent with worshiping the many gods in the Hindu mythological pantheon. These super beings illustrated in books and posters and on big and little screens live in other worlds or in the imagination. But shouldn't we wonder at our imagination? Isn't imagination also a world? Isn't the source of human thoughts and ideas as real as the universe? Isn't the output of the human mind as real as the world which is illusory in itself?

Although Hinduism is a theistic religion, it has many followers who doubt God or ignore God or disbelieve in God. Important schools of philosophy have put forth doctrines that view the human soul independently from God. Because Hindus acknowledge that God is unfathomable, they may freely question, opine upon or dismiss that which is beyond knowing. However, most Hindu atheists and agnostics still believe that good actions and good deeds earn merit and produce good results. Others follow their moral compass with speculation. Hinduism teaches that people who engage in good pursuits without considering merit or results earn the greatest merit. They act with purity because they have no expectations. This perspective recognizes that disbelievers on the path of goodness may progress further than their believing counterparts precisely because they do not have even the expectation of attaining oneness with God.

Hindu philosophy is premised on the idea of God, not on belief in God. Thus the divine force, howsoever it may be perceived, or even if it is disregarded, is ever present. Hinduism does not demand faith in God. Rather it provides links to the idea of God. Those interested can click on a link at any time.

What then describes Hindus if not faith in God, or acceptance of the tenets of Hinduism, or following the dictates of Hindu scriptures, or performing specific rituals? Responses often given to the question "Who is a Hindu?" include: followers of Hindu traditions, believers in Vedic philosophy, persons who follow dharma (a complex inclusive term representing maintaining balance, staying on the path of truth, and fulfillment of duty), persons of righteousness, persons who perform Hindu sacraments, persons who live a Hindu lifestyle, persons who uphold Hindu values, seekers of God, and persons who profess themselves to be Hindu.

The above replies are all correct, but none is definitive, given the wide diversity in individual beliefs. The last statement is probably the closest to the best answer. Nobody can judge the belief of a particular Hindu, but persons who believe themselves to be a

Hindu know what they believe. Thus, a Hindu may best be described as someone who calls himself Hindu and who does not adhere to any other religion.

Hinduism is universal, but distinctive. It is inclusive, but will not incorporate a belief system that excludes freedom of thought. It is a world view that does not accept religions that prescribe exclusive doctrines, mandate specifics beliefs, or disrespect ideas they fail to understand. Thus a Hindu cannot appropriately belong to another faith.

Hindus number about one billion. They staunchly hold to their faith, philosophy, and practices. They have maintained their millennia old traditions at home in India and have taken them all over the globe. Over the years, the Western world has become somewhat more familiar with Hinduism and aspects of Hindu practice like yoga and meditation. More and more people of different heritages are taking interest in, understanding, and incorporating Hindu beliefs into their lives. Some have decided to consider themselves Hindus and if they are good people, they make other Hindus glad.

Notwithstanding the great differences between each Hindu's interpretation of what Hinduism means as a religion and as a philosophy and of what it requires in the way of commitment, it is commitment to their religion and philosophy that defines who they are.

## *Chapter Two*

# Monotheism

Bhagvan [The Lord] said:
"Look! I am in hundreds of thousands
of different forms, and colors and shapes.
Arjun, see in my body, the whole world
and anything else you want to see."

(*Gita* 11:5, 7)

INDUISM SEES GOD as One infinite power.
That power issues forth in countless forms
just like a flame emits countless sparks.
Many of God's forms take on human attributes while
others appear in any form we can envision. The explanation that Hindus believe in One God with many
names is true, but God is beyond names and forms.
God materializes as any aspect of the universe, or of
multiverses. God is everything, though everything is
not God. The world is perpetually changing and moving, subject to the forces of creation, destruction and

regeneration. God is immutable, eternal, untouched by the dimensions that limit the cosmos. God is beyond time and is time itself. In other words, in the universe only God is not illusory. Only God is real and God is the only reality.

Philosophers like to debate the question of whether God created man or man created God. Religions consider God man's Creator whereas science suggests that the natural course of evolution created humanity. But the debate dissolves if we consider God the cause of evolution. Hindus view God as "That" which existed before the universe began and will exist after the universe ends. Hinduism perceives God as the only reality that is not forever in a state of flux. From this perspective, God is the only truth.

The Hindu view that reality is illusory and unreal because it is impermanent has fascinating implications. If the tangible world is unreal, the world of our ideas, thoughts, and imaginations is no more unreal—or less real—than the world we can see and touch. These worlds must be of equal magnitude. Thus, ideas about multiverses as well as multiverses themselves can be real. Collective or individual concepts of god-like beings or demonic creatures may be real. Possibilities like time travel or alien encounters can be realities, foreseeable even for human beings. To accept the idea that reality is fluid and intangible is to accommodate an open ended world view, a world view that can incorporate flights of fancy, one that can extend beyond the present reach of human intelligence.

Belief in the world's illusory nature gives rise to belief in the reality and greatness of nothingness. An understanding of nothingness relates to the understanding of mathematics which embodies the concept of zero. At the same time, belief in nothingness is a significant aspect of Hindu belief in God. Nothingness is greater than creation which comes and goes as worlds appear and disappear in cycles. Nothingness existed before God undertook creation and God alone transcends nothingness. Devout Hindus seek to attain enlightenment which is akin to becoming lost in the supreme blissfulness of God who is as much nothing as He is everything.

Some people revere God as an infinite force requiring no further definition. But others find it difficult to work the idea of an intangible, unfathomable, all powerful God into worship or life. Thus, Hinduism facilitates faith by giving God a multitude of physical forms that represent his multiple attributes. It is next to impossible to know these countless forms and names. In ritual ceremonies, priests recite as many names as the worshipers have patience to repeat or hear while they toss a leaf or a petal for each name into a vessel as a symbol of their acknowledgment.

The original Vedic concept of God is the concept of Brahman. The word Brahman is the Sanskrit root of the noun Brahma, the Creator's name. Brahman precedes the Creator and represents the divine nothingness that anticipated the emergence of matter. The name Ishvar is also God's name. Ishvar succeeds the idea of Brahman. However, Hindus conceive of God as Ishvar in more personal terms. Like Ishvar, Bhagvan refers to God in the absolute sense, but Bhagvan also means Lord and people use the word as a title following God's many names, like "Krishna Bhagvan." "Bhagvan" is the word people usually call out when they pray or say, "Oh my God!"

God is beyond definition, but the Godhead composed of the trinity, Brahma, Vishnu, and Shiva, is definable. The trinity represents different aspects of the single universal God. Brahma is the Creator, Vishnu is the Preserver, and Shiva is the Destroyer. Brahma represents the beginning, Vishnu, the middle, and Shiva the end of the cycles of creation that repeat themselves again and again over the ages.

God as manifested in the trinity possesses distinct visible, tangible, depictable attributes. He has human emotions combined with God power. Brahma, Vishnu, and Shiva and their magnificent consorts, Saraswati, Lakshmi, and Parvati engage in human activities that make them the subject of legends and that endear them to all Hindus, irrespective of their opinion of the universe or their perception of God.

Texts and illustrations portray Brahma, the creator of earth, heaven, skies and beings, as having four heads looking in four directions. We often see Brahma white haired and seated on a lotus or mounting a goose. Brahma, also called Prajapati, Lord of Progeny, is the primordial manifestation of God.

Vishnu, the Preserver of the universe, represents balance and harmony. He has four arms and hands, each holding an emblem of his godliness: the club, the conch, the chakra (wheel), and the lotus. A coiled serpent lies at his feet.

Ten incarnations emanate from Vishnu. The last, Kalki, is yet to come. Rama, Krishna, and Buddha are His seventh, eighth, and ninth incarnations respectively. All three were originally historical personages, though the dates of Lord Rama and Lord Krishna's lives are not established.

Rama and Krishna's stories are told in the two grand Hindu epics, the *Ramayana* and the *Mahabharata*. These works came to full fruition after the Vedic era introduced by the Aryans, but they were centuries in the making. Many components of the epics antedate Aryan predominance in India, be they of Vedic or of indigenous origin. The chronology of the Aryan cultural sweep does not put the age of the Vedic literature at issue because its roots antedate its appearance in India.

Rama, the son of a King, is the hero of the grand *Ramayana*, which tells of his early life, his exile in the forest, and his battle to rescue his wife, Sita, who was abducted to Sri Lanka by the demon Ravana.

Lord Krishna was a cowherd, much beloved from the time he was a baby filled with mischief. He was flutist and a charmer who teased the gopis—milkmaids—and who won the hearts of all whose hearts he touched. Krishna's devotees worship Him with single-minded love, finding ecstasy in simply uttering his name. His dark blue skin comes from absorbing the poison of a five-headed snake he killed. Many worship Radha, Krishna's beloved, as one with Him, because her devotion both controlled and reflected His divinity.

Krishna speaks the *Bhagavad Gita* just before the great war which is the subject of the *Mahabharata* begins. Arjun, the hero of this battle, feels dejected at the prospect of killing his enemies, who are relatives, teachers, and warriors. God urges Arjun to fulfill his duty without worry since the soul is eternal and cannot be killed. Arjun's questions and Lord Krishna's answers crystallize Hindu beliefs and philosophy in seven hundred verses.

Buddha, the Enlightened One, was Lord Vishnu's ninth incarnation. He was born a prince, Siddhartha Gautama, in about 400 BCE or earlier. The place of his birth, Kapilavastu, has not been pinpointed but is believed to have been in India, possibly Nepal. Buddha preached a religion that broke away from orthodox Hinduism and its priests. Buddhism is directed toward salvation rather than worship. The path of Buddhism leads to "Nirvana," a state of eternal bliss and peace which may be equated with the Hindu state of Oneness with God. The Buddhist message is streamlined and focused which makes it appealing even to those who hear it for the first time.

Buddhism was prominent in India for centuries before it evolved into the worship of Buddha Himself and migrated further East. In time, Indian Buddhists lost the support of the royal rulers and converted to back Hinduism. Shankaracharya, who died in 820 CE at the age of thirty-two, won debates with many Buddhist teachers, persuading them and their followers to return to Hindu beliefs. However, Hindus have always respected Buddhism and continue to revere Buddha as the incarnation of Vishnu and as God.

The third member of the trinity, Lord Shiva, the Destroyer, ends time:

I am burning Time, the destroyer of the
world.

(*Gita* 11:32)

Representations of Shiva, also called Maheshvara, often show him sitting cross legged in meditation or else dancing. Shiva is Lord of Dance, Nataraja, and Lord of Animals, Pashupati. He is sexual
energy symbolized by the phallus. The Destroyer is
white in color, has multiple faces and a third eye
filled with visionary and destructive power. The
Ganges River flows from his matted hair, the moon
adorns his head, a cobra garlands his neck, and he
carries the trident.

Shiva's wife, Parvati, is the great mother goddess.
She is the personification of female energy known as
Shakti and revered as the power behind all creation.

God as the force of destruction appears in the *Gita* as
a frightening power beyond reality and beyond unreality. This manifestation induces both terror and ecstasy.
It makes demons flee and saints bow down in awe.

Hindus worship the Godhead, the three-faced holy
trinity, as one absolute God of many aspects. Brahma,
Vishnu, and Shiva are early manifestations of God as
envisioned by man. The Godhead represents the idea
that God's powers are infinite and that they embody
and transcend the universe itself.

The notion of the trinity springs from earliest Hindu thought. Brahma, Vishnu, and Shiva, associated with Earth, Water, and Fire, together symbolize the awesome energy that brings life to matter and spirit to the mind. The Godhead illustrates God force as cosmic force and suggests that understanding cosmic force leads to understanding God and to attaining enlightenment.

Hindu texts contain the oldest documented repository of modern day philosophical and scientific knowledge. Vedic tradition distinguishes eternal unchanging reality, which begins with a breath, from temporal ever changing unreality, which begins with infinitesimal particles of matter. It recognizes the existence of multiverses. Ideas that today float between science and science fiction—precursors of scientific discovery—abound and astound in ancient Hindu scriptures and legends.

In Hindu thought, God alone creates, sustains, and destroys time. God also has the power to expand and contract time. As time cannot be realized apart from God, God is time. Brahma's sleep and wake cycles make time happen. When Brahma sleeps, the universe ceases to be.

> When He awakens, He recreates it.
> Brahma's day lasts a thousand ages
> and Brahma's night lasts a thousand more.

Only the wise
know this truth
about Time.

(*Gita* 8:17)

Hindu astronomical and astrological studies mea-
sure time differently for different worlds and differently again for God. Fine-tuned calculations show
that ancient sages perceived our planet as part of a
much bigger universe or universes or multiverses
brought in and out of being by God. Several parallel
worlds exist with their own space-time on multiple
planes. As humans we have just begun to skirt their
edges but using our minds as vehicles and our calculations as fuel, we have been traveling throughout the
universe for millennia.

Human time is limited. It is short. According to
the ancient Hindu calendar, a human year consists
of 360 days divided into twelve solar months or thirteen lunar months. The lunar months are divided into
fortnights of about 14 days each that are composed of
one waxing and one waning lunar cycle. Two months
make a season and three seasons a semester, or half a
year. Two semesters add up to a year. An extra month
added every third year reconciles the lunar calendar
to the solar calendar.

Ancestral time is the time experienced by our
ancestors who have moved on to other worlds and

other dimensions. Their time lasts much longer than human time. A human fortnight consisting of approximately fourteen days equals one ancestral day. An ancestral year is 5,040 human days. The lifespan of ancestors is one hundred of their years or 504,000 human days which equate to nearly one thousand four hundred human years.

Time experienced in the worlds of gods and demons—superhuman powers endowed with divine and demonic characteristics—is even longer. A human year, calculated as three hundred and sixty human days in the Hindu calendar, equals one day and night cycle for gods and demons. Thus, the one hundred year lifespan of deities and demons adds up to about thirty-six thousand human years.

Far greater than any other time is Brahma's time which Hinduism reckons in *kalpas* or eons that in turn are composed of ages. Hindus have divided Brahma's kalpas into four ages or *yugas* during which cosmic order has consistently deteriorated and human behavior worsened. The yugas become progressively shorter in duration. The earliest yuga lasted over one million, seven hundred thousand years and the current yuga, known as the Kali Yuga which dawned about 3000 BCE is expected to last for only 432,000 years.

According to Hindu cosmology, Brahma undertook creation of the cosmos two kalpas ago. This works out to 8.64 billion years, several billion years less than the estimated age of the universe according to modern science. The most recent scientific calculation estimates that the universe came into being after the big bang about 13.7 billion years ago give or take one hundred and twenty million years.

Hinduism envisions Brahma's existence in terms of billions and even trillions of years. It visualizes the scope of creation as infinite. Modern science has not really spoken on how much longer the universe or world or our planet will last. Nor has it spoken on what its scope may be. It is reasonable to consider these two questions interlinked. The duration of the universe must depend on what it encompasses. The Hindu vision is of a universe that expands and contracts in time and space, one that moves in and out of reality and in and out of consciousness, a universe that dissolves and regenerates itself, that is created by God and that is God. But God is more than the universe. God's greatness is enormous but it can also be miniscule and even if the universe ceases to be, God does not.

Thus, God and creation are as infinitesimal as they are infinite. Vedic wisdom embraces this concept. The *Vedas* call that the briefest unit of time is the *paramanu*. The next unit is a *truti* (a minute fraction of a second) followed by a *vedha* which consists of one hundred trutis. Three vedhas make a *lava* and three lavas, a *nimesha* or blink of the eye. Three blinks constitute a period of eight seconds.

Modern scientific calculation of time begins with a nanosecond, though smaller units are defined. A billion nanoseconds constitute a second. This means a nanosecond is to a second as a second is to 31.7 years. A million microseconds or a thousand milliseconds make up one second. Light travels at the amazing speed of just under one foot per nanosecond, approximately 186,282 miles per second.

According to Vedic calculations, light travels at the speed of twenty-two thousand and two *yojanas* per second. A yojana equals one thousand nine hundred and eighteen miles making the speed of light equal to about 185,822 miles per second, remarkably close to calculations of about 186,000 miles per second made in the late nineteenth century by Michelson and Morley.

The accuracy of ancient Hindu calculations is remarkable, especially since these measurements were probably taken without instruments or techniques that are available to scientists today. More remarkable is the reverence given to the sages that made the calculations and to the endurance of the philosophy that enabled them. Perhaps most remarkable is Hinduism's understanding of the universe it attributes to God's creation and its incorporation of this understanding into scripture.

If science expands and religions contract, a chasm grows between the two. In the centuries following the dark ages in Europe, scientists and teachers who sought to advance their understanding were punished when their views contradicted orthodox religious beliefs. In this the twenty-first century we have not yet eradicated tendencies to deny scientific truth or to forestall scientific inquiry. Hinduism has not entertained a conflict between religion and science. Spirituality and science converge in their desire to know the universe. Hindu philosophy realizes that religion cannot dictate belief or deny the truth as much as science cannot deny that truth lies beyond its reach.

The scientific nature of philosophy and religion and the religious nature of science converge in the concept of zero. Hindu thought has recognized the importance of zero from Vedic times. Even earlier, the Indus Valley Civilization used zero and a decimal system. The Western world, working with Roman numerals, did not incorporate zero into its mathematics until well into the Modern Era when it adopted the so called "Arabic numerals" which came from India.

The Sanskrit word for zero is *sunya* which translates as "nothingness." Brahman, God in his formless, immutable, timeless, memory-less state prior to Creation, is called Nirguna Brahman or Brahman with no attributes. Nirguna Brahma exists in nothingness. With the happening of Creation, Nirguna Brahma becomes Saguna Brahma, the God with attributes who is Ishvar. Zero symbolizes God in nothingness.

Zero added to or subtracted from any number does not change the number. The sum of zero and zero is zero. Zero added to or subtracted from itself remains zero. Multiplied by itself, zero is still zero. However, the addition of zero to the right of any number (without a decimal point) increases it up to infinity and its addition to the left of any number (with a decimal point) decreases it down to the infinitesimal.

Zero's complement must be "everythingness." Everythingness differs from everything just like "nothingness" differs from nothing. The idea of zero embraces the idea of its opposite, totality. We say God is everythingness and nothingness because we have no better words to describe the unfathomable existence or nonexistence that transcends itself. Thus, zero to Hinduism is more than a mathematical tool. It represents God's truth that lies beyond human experience and the material world, truth that is just beyond the reach of the human mind.

The forward march of Science without spiritual awareness is bound to become a self-defeating march, because the more we bite off the pie of knowledge, the bigger the pie becomes leaving our portion

smaller and smaller. The more humankind learns, the
more remains to be learned. As our knowledge of the
universe expands, our understanding contracts. The
better our information, the more apparent become
its flaws. The universe is infinite, but our capacity
to know it is not. The further afield we go to seek
knowledge, the deeper we must probe within ourselves to find it:

> You will see the whole world
> in your heart
> and then in God

> (*Gita* 4:35)

The revolutionary leap science made after Ein-
stein revealed his relativity theory demonstrates how
each answer to a question gives rise to more questions. After moving from a three dimensional spatial model to a four dimensional space-time model,
we have found that many more dimensions like grav-
ity or electromagnetism remain undefined. So far science can only say that the dimensions are out there.
Hinduism agrees. It has acknowledged space-time as
well as the existence of other worlds from the outset.

Hindu chronography measures time in spatial contexts like atomic activity, the blink of an eye, and the
time it takes for the longitudinal angle between the
sun and the moon to increase twelve degrees to constitute a lunar day. Other worlds of super beings and

ancestors follow their own different timetables. These worlds are recognized as real though they must have been actually imagined or explained into existence. The collective mind that gave them substance may be a consciousness, a dimension or even a world in itself.

Hinduism knows much about God, Time, and the Universe. Its ancient teachings have survived the past. What remains to be seen is how far into the future they will propel the present.

The question of where Hinduism acquired its wisdom thousands of years ago intrigues. India's indigenous civilization along with cultures in ancient Greece, Mesopotamia, Sumer, and even the Americas among others suddenly became highly advanced. The Aryans became owners of wisdom that astounds even today. After over two million years of living in the Stone Age, humankind sprung into the Bronze Age as recently as about 2500 BCE. Neither historians nor scientists have been able to tell us how such a massive and widespread cultural jump into a new era came about. We have hints that come from writings many scholars consider science fiction. These writings have made bold suggestions. They propose that aliens came to our planet from the heavens in space ships, that the aliens landed their craft on particularly constructed docks and delivered knowledge that has changed us forever. Could such a thing be true?

Because much can be said about Hinduism, because Hinduism has depth and covers a wide expanse, Hinduism may strike visitors as complex. However, it is simple to those who live within its flexible parameters. It is a religious philosophy that can be reduced to a single syllable: Om. This sacred intonation represents God, Brahman, the Trimurti or holy trinity, the cycles of the Universe, the essence of universality and singularity, the breath of life, and all that is and is to be. Om is Hinduism and Hinduism in its totality is an expansion of Om.

Legends and scripture define Hinduism's scope. Philosophical works probe its essence. Chants of devotees sing its praises. Preachings of gurus explain its guidelines. In these words there is often disagreement. Although the scriptures are preserved intact in crystal clear Sanskrit, they leave much room for interpretation and discussion. The holy writings set forth multiple perspectives and alternate views. People look at different texts or parts of texts from different angles. Translations and commentaries provide further opportunities for proponents of varying mindsets to promote their opinions. However, with respect to the question of one God, the absolute Lord of the universe, there is no disagreement.

Howsoever they describe God, howsoever they see and worship God, whatever symbols and representations they may use to remember God, to whatever extent they doubt God's existence, Hindus and Hinduism contemplate only one Truth and only one God.

## *Chapter Three*

# The Bhagavad Gita

I am God,
the wise,
the everlasting ruler of all.

God is beyond what your mind can understand.
God shines like the sun
far beyond the darkness of ignorance.

(*Gita* 8:8, 9)

THE *VEDAS* CONSTITUTE the core of Hindu Teachings and the *Bhagavad Gita* which translates into Song of God is their essence. The *Gita* is a later Scripture. It is rooted in the earlier *Vedas* and in its time it made Vedic thought contemporary, accessible, and universal. The *Bhagavad Gita* endures today as it is open to interpretation in light of evolving world views. The date of the *Gita* is uncertain but authorities suggest it was put into its present form a little before 500 BCE.

The term *Veda* comes from the Sanskrit word for knowledge. The expression "*The Vedas*" globally refers to the four specific *Vedas* as well as to the explanatory commentaries pertaining to these texts and to other scriptures that embody Vedic or Hindu philosophy and theology. These scriptures are considered divine revelations and are venerated as *sruti,* meaning that which is heard in Sanskrit.

The first two *Vedas* called *Rig Veda* and *Sama Veda* consist of sacred hymns and chants used in ancient sacrificial rituals. The *Sama Veda* is made up of hymns pertaining particularly to rituals involving the use of the deified Soma plant which has hallucinatory properties. The third *Veda*, the *Yajur Veda,* prescribes the manner in which sacrifices should be performed and the fourth, the *Atharva Veda*, consists of metaphysical texts as well as of chants to ward off evil, illness, demons, sorcery, and other troubles that befall humankind. It also incorporates statements about duties required of kings.

The four *Vedas* contain two parts, the *Samhitas,* which are the actual mantras to be chanted and the *Brahmanas,* which are commentaries. The Brahmanas consist of the *Aranyakas* and the *Upanishads.* The *Aranyakas,* or Forest Texts, are designed for use by sages who retire in solitude to the forests to obtain enlightenment. The *Upanishads* are philosophical and mystical meditations. They form the backbone of Hindu wisdom and philosophy. There are over a hundred *Upanishads* some of which are specifically attached to the four *Vedas*. Scholars consider about ten to fifteen principal or primary. These set forth the core tenets of Hindu belief which is Vedic belief. "Hindu" is a geographic term describing the culture that originally developed around the Indus River valley in what is northwest India, Pakistan, and Afghanistan today. The *Vedas* lay the foundation for a religion that teaches and follows *Sanatana Dharma*, the Eternal Law.

The earliest Vedic scriptures already reflect the blend of ritual and philosophy that survives in modern Hindu thought. The belief in One God of many forms emerges in the *Rig Veda*:

> They call him *Indra*, *Mitra*, *Varuna*, *Agni*
> He is heavenly nobly winged *Garutman*.
> To what is One, sages give many a title
> *Agni*, *Yama*, *Matarisvan*.
>
> (*Rig Veda* I.164.46)

The names in the above excerpt represent only a few of the many personifications of gods, forces of nature, demons, examples of animate and inanimate life, and energies worshipped in the *Vedas*. Rivers, fire, mother, the wind, the sun, heavens, divine craftsmen, and death are just a few examples of the super human and extra human entities that blend with God the Creator, Preserver, and Destroyer who is their source.

The attributes, histories, and stories of this multitude of beings overlap and evolve over time making their way into legends, traditions, and philosophy. The vision of the *Vedas* sees every power that fills the universe as impacting mankind. Thus, the scriptures instruct on how to sacrifice in order to appease the powers who exercise control over our well-being. At the same time, the sacrifices are perceived as acts of self-purification. They prepare humans to see the divine spirit whose greatness exceeds that of the universe itself.

The post Vedic texts are known as *smriti*, meaning recollection. This literature complements *sruti*, revelations. Smriti includes law books as well as books about theology, Hindu practice, and philosophy. It stars the two grand epics, the *Ramayana* and the *Mahabharata*. Together the epics have made Hindu Mythology lastingly three dimensional. Over millennia, in stories, in theaters, in books, in movies, or on television, the splendid heroes of these tales have kept audiences on edge with excitement over dramas that unfold and play out causing repercussions that start the cycle all over again.

Lord Krishna preaches the *Bhagavad Gita* just before onset of the Great War that is the subject of the *Mahabharata*. The epic is a recollection, but the *Gita* itself is sruti, a revelation. Each chapter ends

with a statement asserting that the dialog between Lord Krishna and Arjun is part of the *Bhagavad Gita Upanishad*, which is described as "sacred scripture of the knowledge of Brahma and the science of yoga."

This two-pronged characterization of the work accurately indicates that it is both metaphysical and instructive in nature. The scripture of the knowledge of Brahman is a philosophy that helps us understand the idea of God whereas the science of yoga is a discipline that prepares us to experience God. Knowledge and discipline together lay the groundwork for union with the absolute.

The *Gita* is structured as a dialog between God and Arjun. The first chapter describes Arjun on the battlefield facing his enemies. Earlier, both he and his opponents called upon Lord Krishna for help. Krishna offers his entire army to one side and Himself as charioteer to the other. Arjun chooses Lord Krishna. But even with God by his side, Arjun feels dejected and filled with doubt. His mind starts spinning. He sees his wise old uncle, his teacher, and his cousins facing him and he cannot make himself fight:

> How, Krishna, can I fight Bhishma
>    and Drona with arrows on the battlefield?
> I respect them.
> It is better to live as a beggar, but without
>    killing,

because after killing them
our hands will be stained with their red
blood.

(*Gita* 2:5,6)

Lord Krishna's response is the *Gita*. After hearing
God's word, after receiving God's answers to his many
questions, and after seeing God's powers, Arjun is both
humbled and strengthened. He no longer doubts or
fears. He finds faith and courage. He stands ready to
fulfill his duty as a warrior and to fight for his honor:

Lord Krishna,
because of your mercy I know the Truth.
I will be firm and do what you wish.

(*Gita* 18:73)

Arjun's journey from doubt to faith symbolizes
mankind's journey. The journey is premised on a
belief in a principle greater than ourselves and on a
belief that we can ultimately transcend our human
limits. Meanwhile, as we travel on the road to enlightenment, we can improve our human condition. But
the journey must begin with the idea or hope that the
end will have meaning.

God is the *Gita's* premise. Its message is that life's
purpose is to attain enlightenment and eternal bliss
by merging into God. This message is a familiar one.
However its new and concise formulation coalesced

Hindu thought and its fresh expression has guided Hindu behavior into the twenty-first century. In the revelation that is the *Gita,* God delivers His word with beauty and simplicity. This scripture contains eighteen chapters and seven hundred verses upon which uncounted commentaries have been written and continue to be written.

In the course of responding to Arjun, God as Lord Krishna unclouds Arjun's vision, opens his mind and touches his heart. He speaks of His own nature and power, of human nature and human duty, of worlds, of knowledge, of what is knowable, of the universal and human cycles of birth, life, and death and He speaks of truth. Questions related to these matters intersect and overlap and they give rise to further questions and answers. In the end, the *Gita* paints an integrated picture of our human role in the vast scheme of things that is beyond us but not beyond our wonder.

The *Gita* develops around the concept of a universal God who can be envisioned, though not understood on a human level, and around the idea that life's purpose is to attain unity with God. This precept is implicit as are other fundamental beliefs like reincarnation. When the *Gita* makes explicit references to such ideas that are a familiar part of Hinduism, it does so for emphasis or analogy rather than for evaluation. It reiterates them and alludes to them in different contexts, but the beliefs themselves are treated as givens, not as theories. They are considered beyond question, though not beyond interpretation:

> She who always worships God faithfully
> crosses past the world
> and becomes a part of God.
>
> (*Gita* 14:26)

Perhaps the most awesome verses in the *Gita* are those that speak of God's power and grandeur, depicting Him in all aspects and all forms. God is earth, water, fire, air, ether, mind, reason, the seed of all beings, Om, and the Self. God lives in the heart of all living things. Everything that is glorious or brilliant or strong is a spark of His brightness. He is the essence of life. God is Brahma, the Creator who caused the world to be and from whom all things come. He is Vishnu, the Preserver. In this form God is a wonderful sight adorned with jewels and weapons, and heavenly garlands, and covered with fragrant paste. He holds the whole world by just a flicker of His divinity. As the Destroyer, He is Shiva who makes all the worlds afraid. He appears in multiple colored forms. He has large shining eyes and a wide open mouth filled with terrible teeth. His awful brightness burns the universe.

Yet, howsoever the ancients described God millennia ago and however we may visualize God today, the *Bhagavad Gita* explains:

God is beyond what your mind can
understand.
God shines like the sun
far beyond the darkness of ignorance.

(*Gita* 8:8)

Although God cannot be understood by the mind,
God can be known by the spirit. In chapter seven of
the *Gita*, Lord Krishna tells Arjun that he will understand God after knowing Him. God says that He
knows all beings, but they do not know Him. People
cannot see God because confusion and desire cover
their minds, but they can reach God by seeking Him.

The Sanskrit language distinguishes between
spiritual knowledge (seeing, knowing) and ratio-
nal knowledge (understanding). We can come to
know God only by seeking Him. Trying to understand God is a path to knowing Him, yet we cannot
understand God without knowing Him. This is an
apparent paradox, not a real one. It means that we
must take steps toward understanding God in order
to experience God. While the absolute cannot be
understood by our finite mind, it can be known by
our infinite soul. However, the soul can only experience the truth if the mind strives for it to do so.
Reason or understanding is a path that leads to spiritual knowledge, but only spiritual knowledge has
the power to reveal God.

The *Gita* understands God to be both the knower and the known, or that which we wish to know. He is the great soul, the individual soul called *Atman*. He is spirit. God is the knower of the universe and the knower of the "field" which means the human body as well as all embodiment. "Field" refers to place or area, like "field of knowledge." The term field implies that the body is a place where action or conflict occurs. Lord Krishna delivered the *Bhagavad Gita* on the battlefield of Kurukshetra, also known as the field of Dharma or righteousness.

Hinduism sees the body and the mind as one unit, separate and distinct from the soul:

> The body is a collection of many things.
> It is made up of ether, air, fire, water, and
>     earth.
> These are called the five subtle elements.
> The body is also made up of mind
> and the five senses of hearing,
> touching, tasting, and smelling.
> Wanting, hating, happiness, unhappiness,
>     and courage
> are also part of the body.
>
> (*Gita* 13:5, 6)

The mind and body are part of nature and matter rather than an essential or integral part of the God, although God is everywhere. In his manifest form,

God personifies the same subtle elements that make up the body plus mind, reason and the self:

> I am made of earth, water, fire, air,
> ether, mind, reason, and the self.
> These eight things are one side of Me.
> The other, higher side of Me
> is what makes the whole world exist
> and is called the "life principle."

(*Gita* 7:4, 5)

The self when it pertains to the body or to the material aspect of God means ego. It differs from the Self with a capital letter which means the sense of being. The Self is the life principle or the essence of life. It is God unmanifest. It is the spirit that sparks the eternal soul of living beings. It resides within our temporal minds and bodies but it is not of the mind or body.

The concept of reincarnation underpins the Vedic belief that the eternal soul attains salvation by merging into God. A spark of God's marvel illuminates the soul which is confined to the cycle of birth and death until it dissolves into God. When that occurs, the soul's spark becomes one with the flame that is God and the soul experiences total bliss.

Like God, the soul cannot be seen or described or even imagined. It is formless, eternal, and immutable. Until it cuts loose the bonds that tie it to the material

world through self-realization and enlightenment, it
sheds and acquires bodies again and again:

> As a man takes off old clothes
> and changes them for new ones,
> so the soul removes its old body
> and replaces it by a new one.

(*Gita* 2:22)

A person's karma—or self-created destiny—
determines whether the new body that his or her
soul acquires will be born in the world of the wise
and pure or in the lower world in the body of a
senseless deluded being. The *Gita* is a guideline for
uplifting the soul so that it ascends to the world of
higher beings.

The passages in the *Bhagavad Gita* that pertain to the "science of yoga" instruct humankind
on how to better its karma and ultimately attain
enlightenment. They intermingle with the "scripture of knowledge" passages which are philosophical in nature and pertain to the unmanifest world
of spirit. Yoga in its broadest sense means the path
to union with God which can be described as the
joining of individual consciousness to the universal
consciousness. A yogi is a person who has attained
a consciousness that approaches the universal consciousness. Such a person, ruled more by spirit than
by body, is wise.

Many passages in the *Gita* describe yogis and
instruct us on how to become yogis:

> The person whose spirit rules her
>     completely
> is ruled by God.
> This person has self-control.
> She is calm no matter what happens.
> She is calm if she is cold or hot.
> She is calm if she is comfortable or
>     uncomfortable.
> She is calm if she is praised or criticized.
> The person who has self-control never
>     changes.
>
> A piece of stone and gold are the same to her.
> A wise person like this is called a yogi.
>
> (*Gita* 6:6, 7, 8)

A yogi may be a person of action who is detached or
a person of contemplation who meditates upon God:

> A Yogi who is alone
> should find a clean place upon the grass
> and spread a cloth to sit upon.
> Here he should sit and control his mind.
> He should sit up straight
> and look steadily at the tip of his nose,
> not moving at all.
> In this position,

a Yogi must think only of God
until he finds everlasting happiness.
Thinking peacefully of God is called
    meditation.

(*Gita* 6:10, 11, 12, 13, 14, 15)

Only a wise person progresses on the path of self-realization or enlightenment.

The foolish cannot know God.

(*Gita* 15:11)

Fools are those who are ruled by their bodies rather than their spirits. They are slaves to their desires. They are hypocrites. They are deluded. They do not know right from wrong. They are filled with pride and arrogance. Their nature is "demonic" and their destiny is to be born again and again in demonically driven bodies.

Lest Arjun or any person who reads or hears the *Gita* becomes disheartened by fear that he or she may be wicked or foolish, Lord Krishna tells Arjun that he need not worry as he was born with goodness. He tells Arjun and all of us that all our mistakes will be forgiven if we surrender our material desires and give ourselves up to God, the source of protection and peace. God says that whoever hears or reads the sacred dialog between Arjun and Himself is wise. He reveals His secret truth which is that God lives within the heart of all beings. He reassures us once more saying that whoever shares this holy secret with the pure of heart will be sure to come to God. Finally He asks Arjun:

> And now, Oh Arjun, son of Kunti,
> did you keep your mind on everything
> I have said to you?
> Did you understand My message?
> Do you now know the Truth?
> Have your confusion
> and your unhappiness gone away?
>
> (*Gita* 18:72)

Arjun replies:

> Lord Krishna,
> Because of Your mercy I know the Truth.
> I will be firm and do what You wish.
> I will fight!
>
> (*Gita* 18:73)

The *Bhagavad Gita* fills our minds with imagery that corresponds to our emotions and our imagination. It provides something of a road map to help us direct and manage our actions. Perhaps most significantly, it responds to questions that human intelligence cannot answer yet never stops asking. These questions have been posed by philosophers and scientists, by seekers of God and seekers of truth, by people who wonder and by people who doubt. Lord Krishna's answers go beyond what we know, but do not contradict what we know. What His words really tell us is that if we look hard enough and long enough and if we care enough the answers will be revealed.

## Chapter Four

# Paths to God

The Karmayogi does everything for God.
His mind is on God while he acts.
He wakes, sleeps, hears, touches,
smells, speaks, and breathes thinking of God.
He understands that he himself does nothing
but that God does everything through him.
God uses him to get things done.
The person who offers all he does to God
is as untouched by sin as a lotus leaf by water.
The Karmayogi is pure.

(*Gita* 5:6, 7, 8, 9, 10)

YOGA IS THE path which people can follow to become one with God. It is the path of attaining perfection so that we can know God and then merge into Him. A variety of paths can take us to perfection, but they all come together at the end. However, the twists and turns along the way have created many views within Hinduism.

Hindu schools of thought are organized into different systems that go back to Vedic times and continue to evolve and flourish today. The distinctions between them turn on slightly different perspectives of God's nature and of what the best paths to the goal of self-realization may be. Self-realization means finding God within ourselves. It is enlightenment or seeing God's light and becoming freed from the cycle of birth and death. Enlightenment leads to becoming one with the absolute eternal spirit that transcends the universe.

Sometimes the distinctions between the teachings and writings of different swamis (honored religious teachers), gurus, and sages seem esoteric, but these distinctions may influence the beliefs and behavior of their disciples and direct them to seek different paths to liberation.

Teachers and leaders inspire many Hindus with insight and guidance that gives focus to their religious life and to their worship. At the same time these groups are flexible and can intermingle. Many teachings overlap as they all go back to the same scriptures. The Sanskrit texts, though fixed and precise, leave ample room for construction particularly when they are translated into Indian vernacular and foreign languages. Translations and commentaries enable teachers to choose words and draw attention to passages that reflect their own philosophy.

The two largest and broadest groups of Hindus are Shaivites and Vaishnavites, followers of Shiva and followers of Krishna. The differences between the two are philosophical and theoretic. Some people are barely aware of the group to which they belong or to which their family belongs. A third group of Hindus consider themselves primarily Shaktas or followers of Shakti, the Divine Mother Goddess who represents female energy.

Hindu homes often contain an altar which is generally dedicated to the deity worshipped by the family, most usually Lord Krishna, Shiva or one of the many manifestations of the female God force that has various names, like Durga, Lakshmi, or Devi. Shrines and temples dedicated to particular deities may also become regular pilgrimage destinations for devotees. Yet other mainstream Hindus exercise their religion within frameworks like eclecticism, atheism, or secularism without leaving Hinduism's embrace.

Shaivites worship Lord Shiva above other aspects of God. Shiva, the awesome and frightening aspect of God, represents destruction, the force that leads to regeneration. Shiva's energy is also Shakti, the force which is inseparable from female creativity. Shiva Shakti is often perceived as one impersonal, genderless power. Shaivism is monistic or *Advaita* meaning that matter and consciousness are viewed as one in God.

Shiva is probably the earliest manifestation of God that existed in Hinduism. Lord Shiva has been identified with the Rigvedic God of wind and storm who was described as benevolent and kind. The Sanskrit meaning of Shiva is "auspicious." Shiva is thought to have also been worshipped in the Indus Valley Civilization which flourished before the predominance of Aryan culture in India.

Vaishnavites are the largest denomination within Hinduism. Vaishnavites worship the personal form of Lord Vishnu and all his avatars, particularly Lord Krishna and Lord Rama. Their belief merges dualistic *Dvaitism* and with monistic *Advaitism*. Dvaitism views the soul as pure love of God and as separate from consciousness. However, Dvaitist philosophers maintain that the soul and consciousness merge when soul becomes enlightened and frees itself from the body. Thus they consider Bhakti Yoga, or the Yoga of devotion, as the best means of attaining the perfection of spirit that enables the individual soul to become one with the universal soul.

In addition to Hindus, Buddhists, Jains, and Sikhs also believe that life's purpose is salvation from birth and death. Buddhism and Jainism grew out of Hinduism but they rejected aspects of Vedic tradition and developed in different directions. More recently, Sikhism was born as a separate faith. Today these religions continue to share many fundamental principles and values with Hinduism. However, Buddhist, Jain, and Sikh beliefs differ from one another and from Hindu beliefs in significant ways and they follow differently designed pathways to liberation.

Lord Buddha who came to be worshipped as God after his death taught that speculation about the nature of God is futile because God can never be understood. Thus, the purpose of life is to attain Nirvana, the state of enlightenment and freedom from the material world. Buddha preached that we should live by understanding "The Four Noble Truths" and follow "The Eightfold Path." The truths are: the world is full of suffering; desire and attachment cause worldly life; destroying desire and attachment ends the cycle of worldly life; and following the "Way" destroys desire and attachment. The Way is the Eightfold Path: right speech, right action, right living, right effort, right thinking, right meditation, right hopes, and right view. While this path is incorporated in the Hindu paths, the Buddhist way is more crisply defined and presented as a single one without alternatives.

Today Buddhism flourishes primarily outside India whereas Jainism survives as a significant minority religion mainly within the Indian community. Jains do not worship a personalized God, but acknowledge the existence of a perfect universal person. Jainism is believed to have been created by twenty-four Tirthankaras, or Lords, the last one honored by the name Lord Mahavira, meaning great hero. Jain teachings hold that neither creation nor destruction ever existed but that the universe is eternal. It is composed of three realms: heaven, earth, and hell. The heavenly realms contain seven levels of which the highest is reserved for liberated souls. The Jain path to liberation is founded on the three principles of correct faith, correct knowledge, and correct conduct. Jainism believes that the soul can become attached to the tiniest of bodies and therefore we must take great pains to avoid the killing of any creature whatsoever.

Sikhism is the most recent world religion to have sprung from Vedic roots. Today Sikhs number close to thirty million. The Sikh goal of life, like that of the Hindus, is to attain is salvation in the form of union with God. Sikhism understands God as One shapeless, timeless, and sightless being that can be seen only by the heart or inward eye of an enlightened person. The path to enlightenment is meditation and the avoidance of the Five Evils: ego, anger, greed, attachment, and lust. These evils lead to the world of illusion and distance us from the world of Truth. In the beautiful words of words of Guru Nanak (1469–1539), the founder of Sikhism, "Realization of Truth is higher than all else. Higher still is truthful living."

Hinduism as crystallized in the *Bhagavad Gita* teaches three yogas considered the principal paths to self-realization. These are Bhakti Yoga, or the Yoga of Loving Worship, Jnana Yoga, or the Yoga of Knowledge, and Karma Yoga, or the Yoga of Action. Teachers have taken great pains to study Lord Krishna's words and to say that Krishna puts one path above the others. However, Lord Krishna praises all three roads to self-realization and His ultimate message is these paths are one.

With regard to Karma Yoga and Jnana Yoga Arjun asks:

Lord Krishna,
You praise knowing the truth
and then You praise doing good
Please tell me clearly
which of the two is best.
God answered:
Knowledge is knowing truth;
Action is doing good.
Both are excellent paths to god.
But doing good is easier
and so it is best.
The man who does good,
the man who does his duty for God's sake alone
is called a Karma Yogi.
Such a man is also a Sanyasi,
which means a person who has given up
everything for God.

This man is beyond the world and is part of
   God.
Only fools think the paths
of knowledge and learning are separate.
Because a person reaches God by either path.
The wise man understands
that both paths are really one.
He who sees that action and knowledge are
   the same
sees truth.

(*Gita* 5:1, 2, 3, 4, 5)

God similarly praises the path of devoted worship,
repeatedly equating *bhakti*, devoted loving worship,
with detached action:

But by endless love
I can be seen in this four armed form.
By endless love
I can be known.
By endless love
I can be entered into.

(*Gita* 11:53)

But I quickly rescue from birth and death
whoever loves only Me
and does everything for Me only
and worships Me all the time.

(*Gita* 12:7)

The term Yoga is comprehensive. When practiced as a discipline in itself, yoga can be viewed as a channel to God. It is a method of communing with God who resides within our soul. Meditation in particular eliminates the noise of life that muffles our inner spirit. Meditation is known as Raja Yoga, translated as Royal Yoga. It is Yoga of the Mind.

Concentration and steadiness are equally required of those who primarily follow the paths of devotion, action, or worship. Meditation aims at mastering the mind through calmness, unwavering focus, purity, and serenity. These traits are repeatedly lauded in the *Gita* as part of wisdom and virtue. Lord Krishna's emphasis is on practice:

> The Yogi whose mind is concentrating on
> God
> does not shake.
> He is steady
> like a candle in a room where there is no wind.
> The Yogi's mind does not move away from
> the truth.
> To become a Yogi
> you have to practice being calm.
> You have to practice not fidgeting
> and concentrating on God.
> And the Yogi who is perfectly calm
> is pure and free of sin.

He is one with God
and perfectly happy.

(*Gita* 6:21, 22, 23, 24, 25, 26, 27)

More specifically, Raja Yoga is a means to gain
awareness of power that lies coiled like a snake within
our ethereal bodies. The ethereal body is energy rather
than matter. Raja Yoga is based on the belief that we
can tap our formidable spiritual power through centers within us. These centers are sources of energy
known as *kundalini* power. The word kundalini
comes from *kundala*, the Sanskrit word for coil, or
something coiled up like a snake. Seven centers represent higher consciousness. They are called *chakras* or
wheels and are depicted as circles like lotus flowers or
wheels surrounded by petals. These principal chakras
are located from the base of the spine to the top the
head. They are aspects of being that relate to memory,
reason, psychic intuition, decision, inspiration, perception of the inner eye, and ultimately to the attainment of illumination.

Other yogas also promote the balance and well-
being that leads to peace and enhanced consciousness.
Hatha Yoga or Yoga of the Body is widely practiced
today. Other well-known forms of yoga include Mantra Yoga or Yoga of Chanting, Tantra Yoga, an aspect
of Shaktism that worships God as the male and female
creative force, and Vinyasa Yoga that coordinates the

flow of breathing with movement. Generally those who practice yoga combine more than one discipline.

Intellectual analysis and scientific analysis are also paths to higher consciousness. These activities are part of Jnana Yoga, the path of knowing, which is directed toward understanding the absolute soul. Jnana Yoga pursues learning for its own sake in order to understand the universe and perhaps God. In the quest for knowledge, it is important that seekers of knowledge remain humble. Those who study merely for the pleasure of intellectual challenges and who are not attuned to the truths they discover while stimulating their minds, risk losing sight of that which they try to understand.

Hindu philosophical systems suggest yet more pathways or variations of pathways to achieving the perfection needed to attain oneness with the absolute. We can perceive these ways as new curves on the road to knowledge.

Six orthodox schools discuss the major philosophies around which Hinduism developed. These are: *Samkhya, Yoga, Nyaya, Vaisheshika, Purva Mimamsa,* and *Vedanta.* The schools of thought are not mutually exclusive. Rather they are mutually respectful as all pursue self-realization. They all recognize that to reach a higher level of consciousness, people must reach a higher level of perfection. We must become pure enough to clear away the smoke that obscures our soul.

Hindu thinkers envision the absolute soul in different ways and they believe that, although the paths to the truth ultimately converge, they may begin in somewhat different places. The major schools are called *Darshanas*, which means views, or ways of viewing truth. These schools are absorbed into mainstream Hinduism today, but their differences encouraged freedom and diversity to flourish in Hindu thought. The teachings of the Darshanas are the product of intensive and extensive and intelligent analyses of Vedic scriptures.

The dates when the six important schools or Darshanas—meaning visions or viewpoints—became established are uncertain, but they came into existence before the Common Era and evolved over time. Samkhya was the first orthodox Vedic philosophical system to become recognized in Hindu doctrine. It is a dualistic philosophy that sees the spirit as distinct from matter, or the soul as distinct from consciousness which is tied to matter. The soul is pure spirit without characteristics whereas matter possesses qualities that bind the soul to the life cycle. These qualities are called *sattva*, *rajas*, and *tamas* which may be described as balanced truth, passionate activity, and dull inactivity. Liberation occurs when the spirit realizes its separation from matter and disentangles itself from the qualities of matter. Samkhya is associated with the path of Raja Yoga or meditation. In its origin, this system of thought ignored God.

The Yoga school of philosophy is closely connected to Samkhya. Yoga as a Darshana differs from specific yogas which are sciences, disciplines, or pathways to liberation. Patanjali established the Yoga school of thought. He is famous for his commentary on the Sanskrit Grammar written by his guru Panini and for the Yoga Sutras he compiled or possibly, in some cases, wrote. The Yoga Sutras are aphorisms, or short statements mostly about meditation. They number under two hundred but are insightful and persuasive, for example: "Progress in meditation comes swiftly for those who try the hardest." Yoga philosophy encompasses Samkhya philosophy but completes it with God.

The Nyaya and Vaisheshika philosophies are closely related to one another as well. The Nyaya school was founded in about the second century BCE. Nyaya is a system of logic. Its followers believe that the path to liberation is based on obtaining valid knowledge and distinguishing truth from falsehood. Nyaya acknowledges four sources of knowledge: perception/intuition, inference, analogy/comparison, and testimony/word. These criteria determine the validity of the knowledge obtained. Nyaya analysis was used in debates with Buddhism to prove the existence of God.

Vaisheshika philosophy complements Nyaya—into which it ultimately merged—by identifying the objects of perception or experience. They number six plus a significant seventh which is nonexistent or zero. The six objects that can be experienced are substance, quality, activity, generality, particularity, and inherent relationship.

These objects in turn consist of eternal atoms that combine into nine substances: five gross substances which are earth, water, air, fire, and ether plus time space, ego, and mind. The indivisible and indestructible atoms become activated by God's will and creation comes about when souls reunite with particular atoms. God is the force that gives atoms consciousness.

According to the Vaisheshika world view, the universe contains a plurality of souls, each having its individuality which is a consequence of its own deeds. Vaisheshika pluralism has many commonalities with Jainism.

The Purva Mimamsa school was formed to increase focus on dharma in the sense of Vedic rituals. The term *dharma* in Hinduism and its sister religions—Buddhism, Jainism and Sikhism—is important and used in different ways that relate to duty, virtue, right action, and the paths or laws that lead to enlightenment. In the case of Purva Mimamsa, dharma meant the correct performance of rituals with selfless disregard for salvation. Later this school accepted the concept of the Divinity and of attaining salvation through enlightened action. Its philosophy lives today in the meticulous attention that Hinduism pays to the performance of ancient ceremonial rites.

Purva Mimamsa, or earlier school of inquiry, was followed by the *Uttar* or later Mimamsa school that became known as Vedanta. Vedanta incorporates the teachings of previous philosophies. The word Vedanta in Sanskrit means the end or purpose of the *Vedas*. Vedanta also refers to the Bhramanas which consist of commentaries on the *Vedas* and are an integral part of Vedic Literature. Vedanta as a philosophical teaching is a comprehensive school of thought which contains six sub schools: Advaita (non-dualism), Visishtadvaita (qualified non-dualism), Dvaita (dualism), Dvaitadvaita (dualism and non-dualism), Shuddhadvaita (pure non-dualism), and Acintya Bheda Abheda (inconceivable or unimaginable oneness and diversity).

All the sub schools of Vedanta grapple with the question of whether the Universal Soul is separate from individual souls. Advaita or non-dualism maintains that God and the individual soul are the same. They are indistinguishable and inseparable. Dualism holds that the individual soul and the Universal Divine soul are distinct and eternally separated. Pluralism is the belief that the world contains multiple souls that are separate from God who awakens them into consciousness. These philosophies explore the nature and relationship of God to the soul and go to the heart of the question of God's existence.

To ask whether God exists is to ask whether God can be distinguished from that which is not God. It is to ask whether it is possible to distinguish between spirit and matter, between the eternal and the temporal, between truth and falsehood, between reality and illusion, or between existence and nonexistence. By and large Hindu philosophy believes that reason requires us to differentiate true, eternal spirit from temporal, unreal matter. Thus, Hinduism is premised on the existence of a real absolute God and, for millennia, Hindu thinkers have considered the ways God works into our being.

Vedanta inquiry was brought to the United States by Swami Vivekananda, founder of the Vedanta Society, who presented his lecture, "Sisters and Brothers of America," to the Parliament of World Religions in Chicago in 1893. In this speech he quoted from a hymn which he and millions of others repeated daily:

> As the different streams having their sources
>     in different
> paths which men take through different
>     tendencies,
> various though they appear, crooked or
>     straight,
> all lead to Thee.

# *Chapter Five*

# Myths and Legends

God said:
"Look! I am in hundreds of thousands
of different forms, and colors and shapes.
See in me all twelve sons of Aditi,
the eight Vasus,
the eleven Rudras who are gods of destruction, the twins
who are the gods' doctors, the forty-nine
wind gods, and many, many other
wonderful forms never seen before.
Arjun, see in my body, the whole world
and anything else you want to see."

(*Gita* 11:5, 6, 7)

HINDU MYTHS AND legends illustrate Hinduism's world vision in vibrant color. They portray worlds inhabited by people, by super people, by gods and demons, by legendary heroes and evil doers, by fantastic creatures endowed with extraordinary powers, and by great warriors wielding remarkable weapons. These tales tell of places unbound by time or space, places that exist in our imagination, and places we can visit today. They tell of flight through the heavens. They discuss creation and destruction. They speak of God's manifestations and God's power. They bring laughter and tears and they thrill, frighten, comfort, and teach generation after generation of Hindus. Ancient stories told and retold never lose their fascination. They weave themselves into the fabric of Hindu life and take on new life when fresh miracles come about or when nature and science amaze us with feats that we once thought could not be performed outside of our imaginations.

Among the most intriguing narratives in Hindu mythology are the stories related to the ten avatars of Lord Vishnu, the Preserver, in the holy trinity of Brahma, Vishnu, and Shiva. The term avatar is understood to mean incarnation or manifestation, but the actual translation from Sanskrit is "descent." People do not worship all the avatars and all are not human. Hindus adore Rama and Krishna above Vishnu's other incarnations, but Vishnu came as a savior in all of them. Hinduism has consistently viewed Vishnu as the savior. While Brahma is the Creator who starts cosmics and Shiva is the Destroyer who ends them, Vishnu, the Preserver, is the one who strives to maintain cosmic order, intervening whenever needed.

It is interesting to note that the order of the avatars' appearance parallels the sequence of Darwin's theory of evolution. Vishnu's first descent is in the form of a fish, a creature of the water. Matsya saved a ship attempting to escape from a great flood and guided it to safety. The second avatar was in the body of Kurma, a tortoise who restored the nectar of immortality to the gods. The tortoise is a reptile, a life form that followed fish in the evolutionary sequence. Lord Vishnu incarnated for the third time in the body of a land animal, Varaha, the boar. Varaha saved the Earth from the demon who carried her to the bottom of the ocean. After a battle which lasted a thousand years, the boar rescued Earth and restored her to her rightful place in the universe. Narasimha, the giant man lion, was Vishnu's fourth descent and the last which took place in the Satya Yuga, the earliest age in Hindu cosmology. Narasimha symbolizes the emergence of mankind from the animal kingdom. Vishnu manifested in this form to save Prahlada from his father, a demon who was enraged by his son's devotion to Vishnu. Narasimha destroyed the demon and made Prahlada ruler of the earth and the underworld.

The fifth, sixth, and seventh avatars of Vishnu take place in the second age known as the Treta Yuga, a period when man progressed from the stone age, to the iron age and then to a society ruled by kings. Thus, while Vishnu's first four incarnations relate to struggles with demons and the forces of nature, the next three are about social and political struggles among men.

In His fifth incarnation, Vishnu appeared as Vamana, the dwarf who restored heavenly and earthly power to the gods and in his sixth, He appeared as Parashurama, Rama with an ax. His mission was to rid the world of evil and Parashurama went around the world twenty-one times killing bad kings and re-establishing the rule of the virtuous ones. Vishnu's seventh incarnation was as Lord Rama, widely worshipped and glorified in the epic *Ramayana*.

Vishnu's eighth avatar is as Lord Krishna who came to earth to preach the *Bhagavad Gita*. Krishna is probably the most deeply beloved of God's avatars. His descent occurred in the third age known as the Dvapara Yuga. Vishnu's ninth avatar, as Lord Buddha, the Enlightened One, took place in the fourth and current Yuga known as the Kali Yuga. Buddha preached a doctrine of reform that became Buddhism. With Buddha we enter the historic age and await the arrival of the tenth incarnation of Vishnu, Kalki. Millennia ago Kalki was predicted to be a phenomenon who would amaze the world and deliver it from all evil and darkness.

The prophecies describing Lord Vishnu's incarnations became living legends. These legends link Vedic beliefs and perceptions to the present. At the same time they link philosophy to practice and they link moral principles to human behavior. Mythology is prophetic and legends are historic, but the two merge into the panorama that we can see as the stage where humankind acts out its self-made destiny or karma. Hindu myths prophesized miracles that came true, miracles that are yet to come, and miracles that science has explained away. Flying through the skies like birds, in sophisticated machines, was once considered miraculous, but traveling to other planets is now seen as an understandable feat. Who knows what we will see tomorrow?

In September 1995, Hindus all over the world experienced what they considered a modern day miracle. It had to do with Ganesh, the endearing, mouse-riding, elephant-headed deity whom Hindus must always worship before worshipping God. Ganesh or Ganpati is not God, the Absolute Spirit. Rather, Ganpati, like other gods and goddesses in the Hindu pantheon, is a manifestation of certain divine characteristics. God is everywhere and His light shines in all beings, so Hindus may worship Ganesh or any god or goddess or any representation or symbol of God to their heart's content. However, Ganpati is of particular importance because he is the gateway to the absolute God.

Several legends explain how Ganesh/Ganpati got an elephant's head. The most popular one tells that his mother Parvati created him out of the sandalwood paste on her body and of the river Ganges. Then she told him to guard her bathroom while she bathed. Lord Shiva, Parvati's husband, had been away and when he returned he did not recognize his son and was angry at Ganesh for keeping him away from his wife. As a result, Shiva struck off Ganesh's head. Parvati became devastated. To comfort her, Shiva promised to restore Ganesh to life. He told his attendants to bring him the head of any sleeping being they found who was facing north. In a while, the attendants returned with an elephant head which Lord Shiva affixed to Ganesh. Parvati was not consoled. She told Shiva that no one would respect her son with a big elephant head on his shoulders. So, Lord Shiva promised that all worshippers would forever pray to Ganpati before praying to God and would invoke Ganpati's blessings before beginning any important undertaking in life.

In this manner, Ganpati became the leader of people, the lord of success, the remover of obstacles, and the destroyer of evil. He is honored in most Hindu homes and establishments and people celebrate him every year in a big ten-day-long festival held in August or September. True to Shiva's word, Ganpati has become a part of every Hindu's life.

Early in the morning of September 21, 1995, a worshipper in one of New Delhi's largest temples offered a spoonful of milk to a statue of Ganpati. The milk disappeared, apparently absorbed through Ganpati's trunk. News of this occurrence spread and by mid-morning Ganpatis all over North India were drinking milk. By the end of the day and for some days thereafter Hindus worldwide began to test Ganpati statues and they reported that the milk drinking phenomenon was real. The World Hindu Council (VHP) announced that a miracle was happening. The stock market and the federal government closed to allow people to participate in feeding Ganpati statues. Stories poured in from Hindu communities in Singapore, Thailand, Nepal, Dubai, the United Kingdom, Canada, and the USA. Skeptics watched milk disappear, amazed.

Scientists offered an explanation of sorts. They called the disappearance of the milk capillary action which somehow pulled the liquid milk out of the spoon. Other explanations called the phenomenon mass hysteria or hallucination. The milk drinking miracle subsided though reports of some recurrences were made on August 21, 2006 and on other occasions. We may or may not ever know exactly what happened, but there is no doubt that this event adds a new chapter to Hindu legend.

The crown jewels of Hindu mythology are its two grand epics, the *Ramayana* and the *Mahabharata*. These reflect Vishnu's incarnations as Rama and

Krishna. Both epics are literary masterpieces containing a wealth of history, legend, philosophy, and ideology. They are post Vedic works considered smriti or recollection rather than sruti or revelation.

The *Ramayana* was composed by Valmiki, a bandit turned saint and poet. Lord Brahma inspired him to write the *Ramayana*, a dramatic poem consisting of seven books divided into five hundred stanzas and 24,000 verses. It is believed to have been recorded about 500 BCE or earlier. The story is an intricate one with a large cast of characters including gods, demons, humans, super humans, animals, and birds who personify good, evil, or both. The well-developed characters act out their karma with elegance and might. The master plot containing intricate subplots takes many twists and turns and contains many diversions designed to keep its listeners riveted to every adventure and full of anticipation up to the very end.

This epic relates the life story of Rama, the seventh incarnation of Vishnu, and of his wife Sita, a symbol of virtue and devotion. Rama was the eldest and favorite son of King Dasaratha and Crown Prince of Ayodhya. He was designated to become King, but his jealous stepmother Kaikeyi—using a favor saved from the past—forced Dasaratha to exile Rama so her own son Bharat could inherit the kingdom. Bharat himself did not wish this as he was devoted to Rama. Thus, when the Prince left Ayodhya, Bharat put Rama's sandals on the throne as a symbol that Rama would return. King Dasaratha was torn with grief at Rama's departure and died of a broken heart.

Accompanied by his loyal brother Lakshman and his wife Sita, Rama settled in the forest. However, the demon King Ravana, disguised as a poor sage, abducted Sita and flew off with her to his kingdom in Lanka (Sri Lanka, previously Ceylon). He had double motives for the kidnapping: lust and revenge. Sita was beautiful and Ravana loved beautiful women. Additionally, Ravana wanted to avenge his sister, Surpanakha. The demoness had tried to seduce Rama and when she failed she tried to kill Sita. Thus, Lakshman had cut off Surpanakha's nose.

In the skies, the eagle Jatayu heard Sita's cries and proceeded to attack Ravana, hoping to rescue Sita from his clutches. However, in the fight Ravana mortally wounded Jatayu. Still Jatayu managed to inform Rama and Lakshman who then set off to find and rescue Sita. Meanwhile the virile and powerful Ravana did everything possible to win Sita's heart, but she remained steadfast in her devotion to her husband.

As they searched for Sita, Rama and Lakshman came upon Hanuman, the King of the Vanaras. The Vanaras were monkey-like creatures created by God especially to help Rama. Hanuman had extraordinary capabilities and could enlarge himself to gigantic sizes. He and his army went to scout out Lanka where they found Sita and assured her that Rama would follow and save her.

In the course of the great battle that ensued, Rama and his allies defeated the demons and slayed Ravana. They rescued Sita and returned to Ayodhya in a palatial magnificent flying machine. Rama and Sita were crowned in a glorious ceremony. They become parents of twin sons, Luv and Kush. But after all of this, the *Ramayana* has an unhappy ending. Although Rama was convinced of Sita's faithfulness during her captivity, the people of Ayodhya demanded that she walk through fire to prove her purity. She did so unscathed but was so hurt that she called upon Mother Earth for help. Earth opened up and Sita disappeared into her before everyone's eyes. Rama, stricken with grief, walked into the river to join Sita in eternity.

The plot of the *Mahabharata* contains more complexities than that of the *Ramayana*. It was probably completed around the same period as the *Ramayana*, somewhere in the first millennium BCE. It is about four times as long as the *Ramayana*, consisting of approximately one hundred thousand verses. While the *Ramayana* tells stories that highlight the personal virtues, vices, and heroism of its characters, the *Mahabharata* paints a bigger landscape of good and evil. It is the background of the *Bhagavad Gita* which Lord Krishna preaches to Arjun on the symbolic battlefield of duty. The events and stories that lead up to the Great Mahabharata War which is the climax of the epic are structured to prepare minds to understand the message that Krishna delivers to not only to Arjun but also to all who listen to His wisdom.

Vyasa, the author of the *Mahabharata*, was a sage known as one of the immortals. According to Hindu belief, he might still be alive today in some form. Legend has it that when Vyasa was about to compose the epic, Bhrama suggested that Ganesh become his scribe. Thus Ganesh brought his broken tusk to use as a writing instrument. Vyasa dictated and Ganesh recorded the epic.

The theme of the *Mahabharata* is rivalry between the Pandavas and the Kauravas, two sets of cousins who were descended from the same Vyasa who created and dictated this grand epic. The five Pandava brothers—Yudhishtir, Bhim, Arjun, Nikul, and Sahadev—were nominal sons of the deceased Pandu, though actually fathered by five gods. They were born in the forest after the ailing King Pandu left his throne. The Pandavas were not ordinary boys and were said to have been born gleaming with heavenly light. After Pandu's death, the brothers returned with their mother Kunti to Hastinapura, City of Elephants, the capital of their Kingdom. There they found their cousin, Duryodhana on the throne. Duryodhana was the eldest of the one hundred Kauravas, sons of the blind King Dhritarashtra and the eldest descendants of the legendary King Kuru.

Duryodhana was fiercely jealous of the returning Pandavas and of the praises the people of Hastinapura showered upon them, but he pretended to welcome his cousins home. Secretly, he and his brothers plotted their ruin.

The five Pandavas princes grew into fine strong men, notwithstanding the atmosphere of fear and distrust that surrounded them. As Kshatryias, or warriors, they learned the arts of peace as well as the arts of war. They evaded the Kauravas' plots and managed to escape from a fiery building that was intended to burn them in their sleep. To save their lives, they went into hiding.

While in hiding, the Pandavas learned of a contest at which the princess Draupadi would chose her husband. The brothers attended disguised as poor Brahmin priests. The winner of the contest would be the one who could shoot an arrow into the eye of a fish that was spinning on a wheel. Many princes tried and failed. Finally Arjun stepped forward and was successful. Draupadi garlanded him and became his wife. Arjun and his brothers returned to their mother Kunti and told her they had won a prize. Not knowing what had happened, Kunti said that whatever her sons won had to be shared among the five of them and the brothers obeyed. In this manner, Draupadi became the wife of them all.

After a time, the elders at the court advised the Kauravas to make peace with the Pandavas and an agreement was reached. The Kauravas gave their cousins a dry barren piece of land to rule, thinking they would never prosper there. However Yudhishtir, the eldest, had ruled his small kingdom wisely and turned it into a rich and happy place. He built a grand new city, Indraprastha, and made it his capital. In time the Pandavas were able to hold a ceremony known as the Rajasuya Sacrifice which elevated them above all other kings. They invited the Kauravas who could not refuse to attend. But, the more the Kauravas saw of the Pandavas' greatness and wealth, the more their anger grew, and the more they determined to destroy the Pandavas.

Finally Duryodhana hatched a plan. Knowing Yudhishtir would accept his invitation, Duryodhana challenged his cousin to a game of dice. Yudhishtir suspected a scheme, but he loved to gamble and felt that it would be dishonorable to refuse. He also was filled with confidence that he would win. So the Pandavas went to Hastinapura. The day of the game, they entered the new hall that was built especially for the match. Yudhishtir's brother Bhim, his old teacher Drona who

also was the teacher of the Kauravas, and King Dhritarashtra watched silently with heavy hearts.

The game began. Yudhishtir staked a pearl necklace
and lost it. He staked his jewels and lost them. He
staked and lost the gold and silver in his kingdom, his
chariots, his elephants, his horses, his cattle, and his
slaves. He lost all he had, but could not stop. He lost
his kingdom, his freedom, the freedom of his brothers, and finally their wife, Draupadi.

Duryodhana's father, the blind old King Dhritarashtra, saw Draupadi, dishonored before him and
could not bear her misery. He promised to grant her
a boon. Draupadi asked only that she and the Pandavas be freed and that her husbands be granted their
weapons. He gave her what she asked for and, beg-
ging forgiveness for Duryodhana's deeds, he asked the
Pandavas to accept the return of Indraprastha. Thus
the Pandavas set off for home.

When Duryodhana learned what had occurred, he
became furious. He again challenged the Pandavas to
a final game of dice. Even after all that had happened,
and without regard to his brothers' pleas, Yudhishtir
accepted. The five went back to Hastinapura. The last
game was an odd one. If Yudhishtir lost, the Pandavas
would retreat to the forest for twelve years and spend
a thirteenth in disguise. If discovered, the brothers
would spend twelve more years in the forest.

Again, Yudhishtir lost. The Pandavas went to the forest while Duryodhana ruled their kingdom. Twelve years passed and the Pandavas spent their thirteenth year of exile working in the court of their ally, King Virata of the Matsyas. They remained undiscovered, but when they returned and made themselves known, Duryodhana refused to give the Kauravas anything. They were refused even as much land as would cover the point of a needle. Thus the stage was set for war.

The warriors assembled. Lord Krishna offered to give his own army to one side and to give Himself as charioteer to the other. Arjun chose Lord Krishna and Duryodhana chose Krishna's mighty army.

> As Arjun sat in his chariot, watching his
>     army and the army of his enemy,
> his mind started spinning.
> He saw his great wise uncle Bhishma, his
>     teacher Drona,
> the hundred Kauravas who were his
>     cousins,
> and he felt he could not make himself fight
>     them.

(*Gita* paraphrased)

Battle trumpets and conches blared forth and drums reverberated. These powerful sounds shook the Kauravas and they became afraid. Arjun's mind filled with sorrow. He put down his bow and arrows and sat down sadly in the back corner of his chariot.

Lord Krishna preached the *Gita* to Arjun just at that point. Krishna reminded Arjun that he was a kshatriya, a warrior, and that it was his duty to fight a war for a good reason. God explained that if he did not fight, people would think he was afraid, but that if he performed his duty and fought, he would either go to heaven or win victory.

Arjun, heartened by God's words, stood up and the Mahabharata War began. The battle lasted eighteen days and in the end Arjun and the Pandavas were victorious. But the victory was a bitter one. Young and old heroes fought and died with courage. Wise Bhishma, the respected Drona and Arjun's young son Abimanyu fell. Karna, son of Kunti and the sun god, fell too. The mighty and powerful Bhim killed Duryodhana who did not stop hating the Pandavas even at the moment of death.

The five brothers went once again to Hastinapura, their family home, now a sad and empty city. Yudhishtir ruled with wisdom and kindness and as the years passed, the sorrows caused by the terrible war softened.

The vivid lessons of the *Ramayana* and the *Mahabharata* were learned and passed on to generation after generation. These stories show that once the wheels of karma are set into motion, choices become limited. When the deeds and lives of other actors touch ours, their karma intertwines with ours and their acts define our role. All we can do is perform our role with honor.

More or less contemporary with the enthralling epics that dominate Hindu legendry, are the Puranas (old writings). These works elaborate and enlarge the dynamic panorama that is Hinduism's heritage. Perhaps because the Puranas tell many sets of stories rather than a single momentous story, most Hindus do not consider themselves as familiar with them as they are with the *Ramayana* or the *Mahabharata*. Yet, while they may not know much about the Puranas' structure or organization, Hindus probably know more about the content of these texts than they realize. The Puranas are the source of a significant part of general Hindu mythology and legendry. Like the epics, the stories are smriti or recollections. Like the epics they are rooted in the *Vedas* and in India's earlier native culture, but they branch out from these roots. They speak of creation and destruction, of the universe and of time. They trace the genealogies and histories of gods, sages, and kings. They consider the nature and consequences of good and evil. They speak of miracles that may be metaphoric or prophetic or simply beyond our imagination.

Early in the twenty-first century India witnessed an event that some viewed as miraculous: the resurgence of rivers in the desert. Hindu writings make many references to a river that flowed in a region that has been arid for millennia. The *Rig Veda* honors Saraswati as the River, the Mother, and the Goddess. At the time of the *Mahabharata*, it was already known that the Saraswati river had dried up in the desert. Gradually Saraswati, the flowing woman who materialized from Brahma's head, evolved into the goddess of knowledge, music, and the arts.

On January 26, 2001 an earthquake that measured 7.6 on the Richter scale wrought havoc in India. Its epicenter was in the State of Gujarat, but the quakes were felt as far as one thousand miles away. Immediately afterward, a number of rivers sprung forth. One of these rivers began to flow in the arid, salty, and barren thirty thousand square kilometer expanse known as the Rann of Kutch. It measured over one hundred kilometers in length and over eighty meters in width.

Some scientists concluded that the new rivers could be part of the once sacred Saraswati river network that had until then existed only in legends. Others believe that the Indus River which gave its name to the Indus Valley Civilization—that had endured for one thousand five hundred years—was coming back.

The new rivers that were born from the earthquake may not flow above the ground forever. Their waters may not always remain sweet. Yet the resurrection of the rivers has given credence to legends that puzzled many for thousands of years.

## Chapter Six

# Karma and Reincarnation

You and I have passed through many births.
I know them all but you do not remember.
I am born from time to time
whenever the good need my protection.
I am born to destroy the bad and help the good.
My birth is divine and those who understand this
become part of Me
and do not have to be born again.

(*Gita* 4:5, 6, 7)

THE HINDU WORLDVIEW rests upon the principles of karma and reincarnation. These are not interdependent philosophies, but they complement one another to provide answers to questions about the eternity of the soul and man's place in the universe. Karma and reincarnation are not theories in Hinduism, rather they are premises that have evolved along with Hinduism itself. However, it is possible to accept the idea of karma without a belief in reincarnation and vice versa.

Reincarnation and karma may be viewed as reflect-
ing the laws of physics that say "energy cannot be created or destroyed" and "for every action there is an
equal and opposite reaction." In spiritual terms, these
scientific laws imply that the soul is eternal and that
actions have consequences. Thus, Hinduism believes
that the soul is born again and again in different bodies until the effects of its actions are burned enabling
it to join the Absolute Soul that is pure energy.

The earliest Hindu references to reincarnation
describe journeys to other worlds or realms known as
*lokas*. These worlds represent astral planes to which
souls can travel outside of the body after death or
when the body attains different levels of consciousness. At the same time these worlds are viewed as
regions in the universe. Thus, Vedic cosmology sees a
singularity or oneness in the universe that is reflected
in our consciousness. The universe exists beyond us
and within us at the same time. It is a multidimen-
sional and a multitemporal cosmos. Souls migrate
from one world to another and from one body to
another until, after many lifetimes, they yearn to
become free.

Vedic scriptures speak of fourteen worlds. Seven of
the worlds exist on three higher planes: Bhuloka, the
first world or the earthly plane; Antarloka, the second
world or the subtle, astral plane; and Brahmaloka, the

third world or the causal plane of God. These three planes can also be viewed as dimensions.

Bhuloka is the dense outermost dimension of being and consciousness. It is the physical world perceived by the senses. Antarloka is the intermediate dimension, the sphere of gods and higher beings, that exists in between the earthly plane and God's plane. It is a subtle, astral dimension of consciousness. Brahmaloka belongs to Lord Brahma, the Creator. It is both the highest and the innermost dimension. It is pure spirit. Brahmaloka is also known as Karanaloka, the causal plane or as Sivaloka, the plane of Lord Siva the Destroyer who, through destruction, causes a new cycle of creation. To reach this plane is to become entirely absorbed or dissolved in the Divine Spirit and to merge into or become One with the eternal God. To enter Brahmaloka is to end the cycle of birth and death.

The seven lower worlds described in the *Vedas* are located in Naraka, the netherworld belonging to demons and souls that have become distanced from goodness and God. Naraka is the plane of lower consciousness. Its regions are temporary hells of the mind and the universe. They are places where souls may wander for many ages or for just moments. Ancient scriptures accepted the relativity of time and space. Thus, according to Vedic literature the duration of any soul's existence in any world depends upon whether the time experienced by a particular soul expands or contracts and upon the time scales that are in play when souls migrate from world to world.

Hinduism believes that the destination of our soul depends upon our nature at the time of our death. Our nature is made up of different combinations of three attributes or qualities called *gunas* in Sanskrit. These are sattva which is purity and truth, rajas which is desire driven activity, and tamas which is ignorance and inertia. Our actions and aspirations during our life create the sum of the attributes that make up our aura at death and determine what happens to our soul. Lord Krishna in the *Bhagavad Gita* describes the essence of the Hindu understanding of reincarnation in just a few short lines:

> If when we die,
> we are mostly Sattva,
> our spirit gets born again
> in the world of the wise and the pure.
> If we are mostly Rajas,
> our spirit gets born again on earth.
> If we are mostly Tamas,
> our spirit gets born
> in the body of a dumb, ignorant being.

(*Gita* 14:14, 15)

Because the *Gita* and other scriptures consider reincarnation a self-evident doctrine, they do not make arguments to support its truth. This is much the case with most of the doctrines that are a part of sacred Vedic literature. However, philosophers and teachers have made many arguments in support of their perspectives or interpretations of both doctrine and scripture. They have taught that reincarnation explains many things. It explains why some people suffer while others do not or why some children are born with exceptional talent. It accounts for memories and emotions that seem to come out of the blue and it accounts for reports of extraordinary experiences in other dimensions. It accounts for thousands of near death experiences reported by those who went to other realms and returned to tell what they saw and heard. Rather than rejecting these reports because they go beyond what is strictly provable, Hinduism considers many of them truthful and valuable testimony.

Acceptance of reincarnation as a plausible truth helps to connect birth and death by explaining life as an interval between the two. It connects individual consciousness to a universal consciousness. It enables freeing consciousness from the matter that binds it to the limited world of our senses. It visualizes eternity and seeks eternity within. It conceives of multiple dimensions and of transcending these dimensions. It brings ideas about the infinite vastness of time and space to the forefront and it creates wonder at the human capacity to imagine infinity. The idea of reincarnation stretches understanding and opens it to endless possibilities.

Reincarnation is believed to work in different ways somewhat depending upon the world view of the believer. Many religions and philosophies accepted the doctrine of reincarnation in the past and many religions, philosophies, and individuals accept it today. Belief in reincarnation is an integral aspect of Buddhism, Jainism, and Sikhism, faiths that have arisen out of Hinduism. The distinction between the Hindu and Buddhist visions of reincarnation or rebirth is interesting because both beliefs are widespread and subject to diverse interpretation themselves. Lord Buddha's teaching is particularly interesting because His message arises out of His personal experience.

Buddha, which means the Awakened One or the Enlightened One in Sanskrit, began His life as Siddhartha Gautama, a Hindu Prince. After He became Buddha, He disassociated His teaching from orthodox Hinduism. He rejected the authority of Vedic scripture as well as of Vedic ritual controlled by the priests who had to be Brahmins, members of the priestly caste. Buddha preached a Godless view of rebirth. The term "rebirth" represents Buddhist philosophy more accurately than reincarnation.

Although Buddha did not specifically deny the existence of God, He did not accept God as a factor in His philosophy. Similarly, while Buddhism does not refute outright the existence of a personal soul, it holds that the perception of the individual soul as part of the eternal Soul is an illusion. Therefore, while Hinduism believes that our consciousness takes on a new body at reincarnation, Buddhism believes that we get a different consciousness at every rebirth. Hinduism holds that our soul is eternal consciousness, whereas Buddhism holds that it is part of the stream of consciousness.

According to Buddhist thought, the soul does not retain its attributes at death any more than a wave retains its identity when it dissipates in the ocean. An analogy often used to illustrate Buddhism's perspective of the cycle of birth and rebirth is that of a candle that lights another candle as it flickers and becomes extinguished.

Buddhist belief in the process of birth and rebirth is validated by the testimony of Lord Buddha Himself, who upon enlightenment came to know all the details of His hundreds or thousands of past lives. He stated that His present life would be His last. Although Lord Buddha would not include God in His teachings and did not claim to be divine, His followers came to worship Him. Buddhists pay Him homage, if not as God, then as the Enlightened One and Hindus see Buddha as the ninth incarnation of Lord Vishnu, the Preserver.

Most philosophical questions surrounding reincarnation focus on afterlife. However, as the *Gita* reminds us, reincarnation is not just about what happens after death or before birth. It is also a part of the process of ongoing change that begins when the soul embodies at conception and ends when it attains liberation from the karma-caused cycle of birth, death, and rebirth.

> The soul of the little boy,
> the young man, and the old man
> does not change
> even though the body changes.
> And even if the soul moves
> on to another body after the body dies,
> the soul stays the same.

(*Gita* 2:13)

In Sanskrit karma means activity. In religious or philosophical usage, references to karma contain the idea of the fruit of activity. Thus, karma is the law of cause and effect or the law of action and reaction. By improving our karma, we can improve the quality of our present and future lives. By burning our karma, which means exhausting the cycle of action and retribution or reward, we can elevate our consciousness, disentangle our soul from the material world and ultimately become liberated:

> Like a fire burns wood to ashes,
> the fire of knowledge burns the things you
> do to ashes
> and these burnt actions
> give you no punishment and no rewards.
> This is how knowing the truth makes you free.

(*Gita* 4:37, 38)

While Buddhism views liberation without reference to God, theistic Hinduism views liberation as merging into the one Absolute God. Schools of thought that disregard or deny God see salvation as merger into a permanent blissful emptiness or nothingness. However, it may be difficult to separate atheistic or agnostic faith from the faith of those who believe in God but consider God the ultimate and infinite nothingness.

Aside from its connection to the idea of enlightenment or liberation, karma is an ethical standard. As such, it goes beyond the golden rule which tells us to do unto others as we would have them do unto us. Instead, the principle of karma says we should act wisely, without self-interest and in fulfillment of our duty. The karmic golden rule is that we should do unto others what duty mandates. We should follow the path of dharma, the moral and spiritual law that brings about balance and harmony in the universe. Hinduism is known as the Sanatana Dharma, meaning the Eternal Law in Sanskrit. A growing number of Hindus call themselves followers of the Sanatana Dharma, a name they consider more descriptive of their faith than the English word Hinduism. By acting in accordance with the ethical and spiritual discipline prescribed in Sanatana Dharma, we earn merit or good karma that brings future happiness and leads to salvation.

The principle of karma can be illustrated, if not fully understood, by analogy. For example, imagine a shattered window and the presence of many bits of glass on the floor along with a rock some feet away. The action of the rock shattering the glass causes the glass to slow down and stop the stone which we find lying next to the glass, not far away. In this illustration, the workings of cause and effect are obvious and clear. However, karma goes beyond the visible. It pertains to more than just the window, the rock, and the floor. It includes the person who threw the rock, the person who lives in the house with the shattered window, the person who pays for the repairs and so forth. Once set into motion, karma becomes a self-perpetuating and self-extending force.

Another example of the workings of karma is the appearance of diabetes in a person who, for many years, has eaten an excess of sweet foods. In a case like this, the diabetes may come as a shock, particularly to someone who is not aware of the causes and characteristics of his disease. Such a person would not recognize that his ailment or condition is the effect of prior behavior. Moreover, diabetes is not only the result of consuming sugar. It can also be a genetic disorder or a lifestyle disorder. Not everyone who eats many sweets becomes overweight and suffers from diabetes and not everyone who gets diabetes has eaten too much sugar or has a family history of diabetes or has failed to exercise. Diabetes has known and unknown causes, but it is the effect of a cluster of causes and as such it illustrates karmic activity.

These analogies show us that multiple causes may give rise to a single effect or to a bundle of related effects or to seemingly disconnected effects. Karma is like a ripple in a pond. It can expand for a wide area and disturb the peacefulness of all the water contained within its circle. As it spreads, it dissipates until it gets lost in the waters of the pond.

Karma is a force comparable to magnetism or electricity. The laws of magnetism govern the attraction and repulsion of magnetic force and the laws of electricity govern interaction between electrically charged particles. The law of karma governs causality between moving forces. Human beings activate karma at the same time that we are subject to its power.

We attract and repel at the same time that we are subject to attraction and repulsion. Our minds create energy at the same time that we are subject to electric force. We make our karma and are subject to its effects. Like other cosmic principles, karma applies to the infinite as well as to the infinitesimal universe. It applies to mountains and oceans, to living beings and to the tiniest cell, to planets and to atoms, to thoughts and to deeds.

Hinduism recognizes three or four types of karma, depending upon how they are grouped or combined: Sanchita Karma, Prarabdha Karma, Kriyamana Karma, and Agami Karma. These classifications relate to the time frame in which the karma or causation was accrued and the time frame in which its effects are realized. Regardless of how it may be classified, all karma flows on and blends into new karma until the soul to which it is attached attains enlightenment.

The accrual of karma can be likened to the accrual of profit and loss in the accounting of our lives.

Sanchita Karma is the sum total of the unresolved karma accumulated in past lives. This is the karma that we bring from our past existences into our present existence. It determines things like the qualities with which we are born and the families into which we are born as well as the time and place of our birth which establish astrological influences in our lives.

Sanchita Karma continues to accrue in our current life since, once we have acted, our present actions become part of our past.

Sanchita Karma or accumulated karma is karma that we have not yet burned. Until it is exhausted, it continues to generate more karma and to cause ongoing birth and rebirth. Hindu teachers tell us that we can reduce the effect of Sanchita Karma through various methods of self-purification. We can follow one of the three paths to enlightenment: performing good action (which means selfless action), seeking good knowledge (which means true knowledge), or worshipping God faithfully (which means sincere, consistent worship). Or we can attain a higher level of consciousness by practicing yoga and meditation or by faithfully performing sacrificial acts.

According to the *Bhagavad Gita*, we can reach God by loving God, by acting with purity in doing our duty, and by learning the truth. Knowledge is a boat that takes us across the ocean of ignorance to God. Knowledge is the fire that burns our karma. It is the sword that cuts out doubt. Knowing the truth releases the bond that binds our soul to the material world and frees us from the endless cycle of birth, death, and rebirth:

> But I quickly rescue from birth and death
> whoever loves only Me

and does everything for Me only
and worships Me all the time

(*Gita* 12:6)

Oh Arjun, do everything for God's sake.
The doubt in your heart
is the doubt of not knowing the truth.
With the sword of knowledge, cut this
      doubt out.
Be free.
Do your duty for God's sake.
Stand up and fight!

(*Gita* 41, 42)

Prarabdha Karma is the part of our karma that is
destined to ripen and bear fruit in our present life.
As it has already been set into motion, it cannot be
stopped or erased. Prarabdha Karma is selected from
Sanchita Karma to be experienced in full during our
current life span. It is like a gain or loss carried forward that expires at our death. Prarabdha Karma is
the sum of causes that arose over past lives but will
yield effects in this one. This karma determines how
our present life will unfold. It is a reason why bad
things happen to good people and good things happen to bad people.

Kriyamana Karma is karma that we create in this
lifetime for the future. It is leashed by the actions we

perform and the decisions we make. Kriyamana Karma is a function of our free will. It is within our control. This is fresh karma that may become exhausted during our lifetime or may be carried forward into future lives. Kriyamana Karma consists of two parts. The part that bears fruit and completes itself right away is called Arabdha Karma, or karma that has begun to take effect. It is viewed as a seed on the verge of sprouting. The result of a good act in the process of being rewarded or a bad act in the process of being punished is Arabdha Karma. The part of Kriyamana Karma that remains pending and will not bear fruit until future lifetimes is Anarabdha Karma, or "unbegun" karma. It is karma that is not yet ready to work itself out. It is viewed as a seed that was planted but stays dormant. A good act that remains unrewarded or a bad act that remains unpunished and neither repented nor atoned for in our lifetime is Anarabdha Karma.

A fourth type of karma, Agami Karma, is sometimes grouped with Prarabdha Karma and sometimes with Kriyamana Karma. The portion of Agami Karma we generated in the past, is Prarabdha Karma, over which we have no control. The portion we generate in the present is Kriyamana Karma. However, Agami Karma is not completely within our control. We create it by making choices that are influenced by our nature, by chance or by other previously determined factors. Agami Karma causes the decisions we make about things like whom we marry, how educated we become, and what we make our priorities in life. The effects of these decisions cannot be resolved in our present lifetime. They linger into future lifetimes as Sanchita Karma or the sum total of our karma. Agami Karma could be viewed as a seed that was planted in the past, is tended in the present, and will become fruitful in the future.

Vedic philosophy and Hindu teachers explain karma in terms of archery. All the arrows in our possession represent our Sanchita Karma. They are all parts of the cumulative karma that we must exhaust or burn to become freed from the cycle of reincarnation. The arrows that we shoot into the air represent our Prarabdha Karma. They are arrows that we already set into motion. They cannot be stopped. The arrow that is in our hand, about to be unleashed, represents Kriyamana Karma. We can control whether or not we shoot it and where we aim it. The accuracy and reach of our aim are our Agami Karma. Factors beyond our control, like how well we aim and how far we can shoot, decide how close we come to hitting our mark. Eyesight, coordination, inherent tendencies like perseverance, opportunity, and chance events, like an unexpected wind, all determine where our arrow falls.

It is symbolic that Lord Krishna preaches the *Gita* on the battlefield, known as the Battlefield of

Dharma, or the battlefield of duty where the weapons are bows and arrows. Arjun, the leader and hero of his army, cannot bring himself to unleash the arrows he holds in his hand. Both Arjun's army and the army of his enemy stand ready to fight. The chariots are assembled. Both armies have called the battle cries. Suddenly, Arjun is struck by sadness. He speaks to Lord Krishna who is his charioteer:

> My bow is dropping out of my hand.
> My skin is burning.
> My mind is spinning.
> I cannot stand up.

> (*Gita* 1:30)

According to Hinduism, God does not cause karma, but He implements or dispenses it. In the *Gita*, God explains to Arjun that the death of his enemy is already decided. Their karma has already been determined, although Arjun's karma has not. God explains that whether or not Arjun kills his foe, they will be killed. Those about to be killed have already caused their own destruction, but Arjun still holds his karma in his hands. It will depend on his decision. He must choose whether he will be God's instrument or not:

> All your enemies will not live, Arjun,
> even though you yourself do not kill them.
> These warriors, your enemies, will be killed
>     by Me,

God, not by you.

I am just using you, Arjun, to destroy them.

(*Gita* 11:33, 34)

Arjun has two choices: to fight or not to fight. Lord Krishna tells Arjun that if he does not fight, he will be viewed as a coward, that his shame will be worse than death, and that he will fail in his duty. But, if he fights, he will fulfill his duty, win glory and go to God, whether he lives or dies. God says:

You are lucky to have a chance to fight in
　　this war
for your duty will take you to God.
And if you do not fight,
you will be giving up your duty.
Giving up duty is a sin.

(*Gita* 2:32, 33)

We make our karma and God makes it happen. Yet God, the Absolute Spirit, is beyond karma and beyond the cycle of birth, death and rebirth. He is beyond the Universe that He creates, destroys and recreates again and again.

## Chapter Seven

# Rituals and Traditions

Now you know.
You know that you should do
what the holy books say
is right and good.

(*Gita* 16:24)

THE *VEDAS* PRESCRIBE the manner in which ceremonies, known as *pujas*, should be performed. The earliest described sacrificial rituals were undertaken to appease forces of nature, spirits, demons, and gods. Later they evolved into rituals dedicated to the worship of the absolute God. Today pujas remain an important center of Hindu life. They are festive events where God is respectfully given offerings of sweetmeats, fruit, flowers, and incense. At large ceremonies, participants and visitors dressed in their finest clothes and adorned with jewelry come to homes and temples in happy moods.

Most attendees enjoy worshipping with their friends and family and then sharing the treats that follow. They are attentive to the proceedings for a while, but not bound to absolute silence and many hope that the priest will move things along at a brisk pace.

An entire Veda, the Sama Veda, was dedicated to ceremonies in which the cannabis-like soma plant, similar to marijuana, was honored and used to modify states of consciousness. While partaking of this plant, ground up in milk or mixed into food, is no longer a current practice, the puja is still meant to be a pleasurable experience that brings about feelings of well-being.

Religious ceremonies, whether elaborate or simple, belong to Hinduism's living and growing memory. Long standing cultural practices that link the present to the past become tradition. The practices of some persons reflect strong beliefs whereas those of others are more of habit. Certain traditions, like arranged marriage, have enduring effects while others, like eating sweets before undertaking a journey, are symbolic gestures. It may take a great deal of effort to follow some traditions, like learning the language of one's ancestors, or giving up meat, or going on distant pilgrimages. On the other hand, following other traditions, like wearing a particular gem stone for good luck, can be easy, enjoyable, or comforting.

Traditional practices among Hindus vary from person to person, from family to family, from region to region, and from one community to another. One could say that each Hindu follows a self-designed path that becomes his or her personal tradition. Although traditions are well established, they adapt to the times and circumstances. In the past, Hindu joint families were the norm. Work was passed down from father to son and a family was like a small commune where everyone worked for the common good. Now, in India and worldwide joint Hindu families are breaking up and nuclear families are increasing in number. Children develop different skills and travel to study and to find work. Opportunities for a joint family to thrive as a single economic unit are becoming limited and less inclination exists to participate in a lifestyle that does not afford much privacy.

While Hindu practices are not cast in concrete, the beliefs underlying the practices have remained stable over the ages. People find the means to uphold traditions and to pass them along to successive generations. Hindus seek out lessons, classes, teachers, and media programs that reach out and teach the young new ways to preserve old ideals and ideas. Like-minded friends gather together and make purposeful efforts to preserve their valuable heritage and to pass it along to their children.

Hindu traditions touch most aspects of daily life. Language, dress, use of symbolic markings like a dot on the forehead or red powder in the hair parting, wearing the sacred thread or special bracelets, greeting others in a particular manner, praying , engaging in meditation or yoga, following astrological recommendations, observing dietary restrictions or fasts, respecting certain superstitions, visiting temples and shrines, or using particular Hindu names are some of the many traditions that are a part of Hindu life. People follow some traditions wholly and consistently while they follow others in part or from time to time. Not everyone in a family observes the same traditions, as not everyone finds every tradition relevant to his or her personal values or beliefs. However, everyone is expected to respect the traditions that their loved ones do observe.

Many Hindu traditions have multiple meanings. A good illustration is the dot often seen on women's foreheads. Traditionally both men and women wore a red dot, known as a *bindi* or *tikka*, in between their eyebrows. Priests still bless participants in ceremonial worship by putting a tikka on their brows. They use *sindoor*, a powder made of dried turmeric mixed with lime, that turns deep red. Mixed with water, the powder becomes a paste. The priest applies it with his finger tip so it is round.

From a philosophical viewpoint, this dot, represents a third eye that has mystical meaning in both

Hinduism and Buddhism. It symbolizes spiritual vision. The third universal eye can look inward and see what our two real eyes cannot.

For millennia, Hindu girls and women have worn a bindi as a blessing and as a symbol of marriage. Many women remove it at the death of their husband, so a bindi may also indicate that a woman has a living husband. The bindi or tikka is a sign that a person is Hindu or respects Hinduism. Today women use a tikka like a beauty mark. It is unlikely to be made of paste and it may not even be red. The mark could be square or mango-shaped and it may be a plastic "stickie" that matches the clothes a woman is wearing. It may sparkle or be layered in different colors. It can be made with lipstick or liquid, or with the traditional dried powder that sticks on with wax. The same red powder that is used in making a bindi is used by many married Hindu women in the parting of their hair.

Vegetarianism is also a Hindu tradition, although historically meat eating has been acceptable, especially in northern cooler climates. At the same time, abstinence from meat is praised based on several principles. Hinduism maintains that eating meat lowers one's level of consciousness and is detrimental to spiritual development. In general, moderation and abstinence from certain foods are seen as a discipline that purifies the body and the mind both physically and spiritually. Thus, avoiding meat is viewed as a good thing that improves our sense of well-being. Many Hindus not only avoid meat, but also observe fasts or keep diets that are salt and grain free on certain days. Another important reason for vegetarianism is to prevent the purposeless killing of innocent animals, which is considered violent and wrong, even though it is known that in early Vedic times sages engaged in animal sacrifice.

A later Vedic text, the Laws of Manu or Manusmriti, allows eating meat under certain circumstances, but prohibits it under others:

> The eater who, even daily,
> eats what is destined to be his food,
> commits no sin for the Creator himself
> created both eaters and those to be eaten.
>
> (*Manusmriti* 5:30)

> There is no greater sin than that of a man
> who, though not worshiping God or
>     ancestors,
> seeks to increase the bulk of his own flesh
> by eating the flesh of other beings
>
> (*Manusmriti* 5:52)

The *Laws of Manu* were written at the start of the Common Era. These laws describe Hindu society and prescribe what Manu, its legendary author, or its actual compiler believed was or should be the norm. The *Manusmriti* contains a wealth of trivia as well as important information that gives insight into the traditions of the times. It delves into minute detail about many aspects of daily life, from recommending what name to give a woman (one that does not imply anything dreadful, that is pleasing and ends in a long vowel, *Manusmriti*, chapter 2, verse 33) to warning that a man who seeks another's wife will be reborn as a demon (*Manusmriti*, chapter 2, verse 33).

The *Manusmriti* is criticized today primarily because it upholds the caste system that is no longer permissible by law in India and because it holds men and women to different standards. At the same time, we should note that this work speaks of and to a segment of a culture that prevailed thousands of years ago. Even in its day, it was treated as a recollection, smriti, rather than as a revelation or sruti.

Hindu vegetarians are significantly conditioned by Jainism which allows absolutely no killing of even the most minute being. The strictest vegetarians tend to come from regions where Jains are most influential. However, along coastal areas and particularly in the East, vegetarians who would not eat even cake because it contains eggs, eat fish in abundance.

Jainism and Buddhism strengthened the Hindu reluctance to slaughter cows and eat beef. Restrictions against this practice are believed to have arisen a few hundred years before the Common Era. At that time, the cow became increasingly important as people depended upon milk and milk products for nourishment and upon the labor of bulls and oxen for agriculture and for transport. Hindus do not worship cows or consider them deities, but they do revere and love them and hence shelter them from harm.

Marriage is virtually required by traditional Hindu society, which idealizes family life. The state of marriage is intended to be a vehicle for joy and harmony as well as for procreation and for the fulfillment of filial duty. Though ancient myths and legends speak of polygamy and polyandry, today Hindu marriage is monogamous. The *Ramayana* speaks of jealousy between wives and the *Mahabharata* tells the story of Draupadi who was married to five husbands. Polygamy was customary in the times the myths and epics were first told and polyandry, though more limited, existed as well. These customs have not survived. Today orthodox Hinduism considers marriage as the joining of one man and one woman. However, the sacred wedding ceremony continues to unite not just the bride and the bride groom, but their families as well.

The *Manusmriti* acknowledges, though it does not condone, eight kinds of marriage: where the father gives the daughter away to a carefully chosen learned man; where the father gives his daughter to a priest out of gratitude; where the bride's father gives her away in exchange for the gift of a cow and a bull; where the father gives his daughter away with a blessing; where the bride and bridegroom secretly elope; where the groom pays the bride's relatives and takes her away; where the groom abducts the bride; and where the groom seduces a girl who is intoxicated or sleeping or otherwise unable to consent and then marries her.

The first type of marriage was considered the best and this arrangement survives, with modification, into the present. Some of the other kinds of marriage also keep happening as they reflect human nature and cannot really be stopped. In the past, parents arranged their children's marriage without any involvement on the part of the bride and groom. Marriages worked out more often than not since the spouses were deeply committed. Happiness depended on chance and on the due diligence done by parents and relatives. It helped that the bride and groom were young, flexible, at their biological prime, and eager to enjoy the pleasures of being wed. It also helped that they were supported by large families and not yet burdened with responsibility.

Today, particularly in urban areas and among the educated, marriages are postponed for social, economic, and personal reasons. Young people are exposed to options and make their own decisions. As young men and women mature, they become more selective and less flexible. Their parents press harder and harder for marriage. Sooner or later the still single young people, often professionals, who have not found a mate in school or in their social circle begin to accept the intervention of their parents and relatives. Often those who are away from India cannot find a compatible partner with shared values who is acceptable to them. Thus, they agree to introductions and eventually to a marriage based on a meeting that has been arranged or set up. Sometimes the marriage takes place quite soon after the initial meeting. Again, the success of these marriages depends on chance, on character, on honesty, and on the due diligence that was done to avoid disagreeable surprises. While today's couples may not have the benefits of youth or of freedom from responsibility, they do have commitment and the bride and groom hope for happiness knowing they started off with a choice and with the blessings of their elders.

In the past, astrological compatibility was often considered in the selection of a mate. While it seems that less importance is given to birth charts today, the date of the wedding ceremony will almost certainly be selected with astrology in mind. While not all Hindus believe in the influence of the planets and their movements, most of them prefer to play it safe, particularly when it comes to something simple like a choosing a date. Not to marry someone we love because of a horoscope that may or may not be accurate can seem unreasonable. On the other hand, most people think nothing is lost by starting a new job or purchasing of a new car, or breaking ground for a new construction on an auspicious day. And most Hindus believe they have nothing to lose and everything to gain by asking that their new venture be blessed.

The Hindu community celebrates most important events in life by invoking the blessings of God, of elders and of powers that are greater than their own. They may hold an elaborate ceremony, or they may privately pray over their undertaking by joining their hands and bowing their heads to remember God, or they may just dip their finger in red powder and write Om, God's universal symbol, on the walls of their new home.

Many families worship daily at a home shrine which may be placed in a corner of a room or occupy a room of its own. One member of the family performs a daily *puja* to pray and establish connection with God as well as to bless the home and those who live in it. The family sets up an altar with an image of the deity that they love the most. Fresh flowers adorn the shrine and incense is lit. At the puja, the worshipper symbolically washes the deity's feet, adorns it with a tikka and offers water and a drink made of five nectars known as *panchamrit*: milk, curds, honey, ghee (clarified butter) and sugar. Fruit or a sweet is placed before the deity to be blessed. Finally the worshipper does the *arti*. He or she ignites a wick, circles it before God's image, and rings a bell, chanting God's name. The small flame or *diya* represents the light of knowledge. After the arti, worshippers symbolically place their hands above the flame and then cover their eyes to partake of spiritual enlightenment.

While all pujas follow this pattern, ceremonies that are performed for particular reasons contain additional and expanded rituals. Pujas are performed to mark rites of passage, to give thanks for specific or general good fortune, to bring good energy to the home, and to celebrate festivals, holy days, and special occasions.

The major life events that traditionally are celebrated with ceremonies include name giving when the child is from eleven to forty days old, the *mundan* or first shaving of a child's head generally before the child is three years of age, the *janoi* or giving of the sacred thread to a boy usually after the age of about nine, then marriage and finally death. Some families chose to hold ceremonies to mark and bless other events like pregnancy, the first offering of solid food to a baby, ear piercing, or engagement. Celebratory pujas for all these occasions may be held in the home, in a temple, or in a public place.

A baby's name giving ceremony can be a simple private affair or it can be turned into a large celebration. The baby is welcomed and everyone present prays for the new little girl or boy to have a happy, long, and good life. After the chosen name is offered to God to be blessed, the father whispers it in the baby's right ear.

The first haircut is the next big event in many Hindu families. Generally the child's hair is allowed to grow, untrimmed, until the family is ready to get it shaved off. The shaving of hair represents the shedding of ego. As this ceremony usually takes place when a child emerges from babyhood into childhood it is a milestone that most parents are eager to share.

Receiving the sacred thread is a significant milestone in the life of a boy. It traditionally marked the time he began to study the *Vedas* with his guru. Today this ritual symbolizes the beginning of maturity and spiritual awareness. At this ceremony, a priest gives the boy being honored a sacred thread to be worn over the left shoulder. The boy's parents teach him the

Gayatri Mantra, a beautiful chant from the *Rig Veda* which must be repeated three times.

The Gayatri Mantra, dedicated to the Goddess Gayatri, Mother of the *Vedas*, is one of the most important chants in Hinduism. This mantra expresses the essence of the *Vedas*. It contains only fourteen syllables, but its compact, complex eloquence is difficult to express in languages other than Sanskrit. It means:

Om
Truth
Earth
Air
Heaven
May the Brilliant Glory
of the Supreme God
Enlighten Our Minds
Enlighten Our Thoughts
Enlighten Our Meditation

(*Rig Veda* III.62.10)

The initial wearing of the sacred janoi, a nine stranded cotton thread, and learning the Gayatri Mantra is an initiation into the world of learned and pious men. The young boy who puts it on for the first time becomes "twice born." In the past, persons who received the sacred thread wore it for the rest of their lives, exchanging it for a new one at an annual ceremony performed near a body of water. However, men and boys of the last generation or two are comfortable with letting it rest in a drawer. But these same boys and men rarely forget the Gayatri Mantra.

Wedding ceremonies probably capture more attention than any other Hindu ritual. These are grand and colorful events that take place over many days. By and large, Hindu weddings have not trended toward simplification. They last for at least several days since festivities and ceremonies begin well before the actual wedding itself. Some ceremonies pertain to the bride, some to the groom, and some to both. The rituals generally include a puja to Lord Ganesh, the elephant-headed deity who is always worshipped before any other worship can be performed, and a puja to calm astrological influences and invoke positive energies.

It is customary before the wedding for girlfriends and female relatives to gather around the bride at the decorating of her hands and feet with intricate henna designs. This cheerful ceremony is called the *mendi*. While the bride is being adorned, the groom's family and friends are often busy covering him with a cool and fragrant paste made of sandalwood and turmeric.

The biggest pre-wedding event is the Sangeet, a music and dance party given by the bride's family to entertain the groom and his family as well as their own inner circle of friends. The Sangeet, or concert, begins with a brief ceremonial bestowing of blessings. A well-planned program and a good meal follow the blessing. Amusing speeches, home created comedy sketches, or professional musicians and dancers may be part of the lighthearted show.

The actual wedding usually takes place a day or two after the Sangeet. It is an elaborate event for which some families save for years. The traditional wedding begins with the arrival of the wedding procession. A drummer's band heralds their approach. The groom, decked out in a turban or wearing other finery, may come mounted on a horse, or in a vehicle decorated with flowers, or even on an elephant. The groom's family and friends surround him.

The bride's family greet, honor, and garland the groom and his family. They serve them sweets and a beverage before leading the groom to the canopied wedding platform known as a *mandap*. Then the bride, bejeweled, dramatically coifed, and dressed in red and gold silks, is brought in by her relatives. Sometimes she is carried on a palanquin. The couple is seated, separated by a cloth. In the course of the ceremony, the cloth is removed and the bride and groom garland one another. The actual moment of marriage occurs when the bride and groom, hand in hand and in the presence of witnesses, take seven steps around the sacred fire.

With each of the seven steps, the bride and groom make an invocation to God on one another's behalf. The chanted prayers are addressed to God in the form of Vishnu, The Preserver. They are simple, but priests explain and elaborate upon them, often tweaking their commentaries to conform to the bride and groom's request or to their own views. The same chant is repeated seven times with a different ending. These seven prayers essentially say:

> May the Great Lord Vishnu follow each one of your steps so that you may prosper and provide for your family.

> May the Great Lord Vishnu follow each one of your steps so that you may attain excellent physical, mental, and spiritual well-being.

> May the Great Lord Vishnu follow each one of your steps so that you may perform your rituals righteously and your faith may grow.

> May the Great Lord Vishnu follow each one of your steps so that you may righteously obtain knowledge, happiness and harmony.

> May the Great Lord Vishnu follow each one of your steps so that you may promote the

welfare of your dependents and be blessed with noble children.

May the Great Lord Vishnu follow each one of your steps so that we may share many bountiful seasons.

May the Great Lord Vishnu follow each one of your steps so that your worship may be fruitful and free from interference.

At the completion of the seventh step the bride and groom promise to be true and faithful to one another, to provide companionship to one another, and to be the best of friends forever.

Throughout the wedding ceremony the bride and bridegroom are barefoot and this offers an opportunity for some fun. Traditionally the bride's sisters and cousins take away the groom's shoes and hide them. They then offer to return them to the groom, for a price. Negotiations for the return of shoes are intense, but finally an agreement is reached and the sisters give them back.

The final stage of the wedding ceremony is the farewell, known as the *vidai* or send off. The bride's family formally bids her farewell and she leaves to begin a new life as part of her husband's family. This is invariably a tearful event and even if the bride and her family are not sad, they well up with emotion.

At the same time, everyone feels a sense of relief that the wedding has gone well or that glitches have been overcome. However, the wedding may not be really over, because the reception is yet to come.

Along with ceremonies that mark transitions, Hindus consider the Satyanarayan Katha or Satyanarayan Puja an important ritual that honors Satyanarayan, a form of Lord Vishnu. The word *katha* means story. Most people perform this ceremony many times in life, particularly whenever a wish is fulfilled or an important plan bears fruit.

The puja begins with the story of its origin. It is said that the sage Narad Muni or Giver of Wisdom once approached Lord Vishnu and asked Him how to relieve mankind from suffering. Lord Vishnu replied that anyone who fasted and then performed a puja to worship Satyanarayan would receive an abundance of life's pleasures, would be relieved from suffering, and would attain his goals.

Following this introduction, the ceremony tells four stories. One is about a Brahmin, two are about a merchant, and one is about a king. All had promised to perform the Satyanarayan Katha but failed to do so and were struck with many woes. However, the stories all end happily after the puja is performed. Each segment of the katha ends with the words, "Satyanarayan Dev Ki Jai," meaning "Praised be Lord Satyanarayan."

The first tale is about a poor Brahmin. One day, God disguised as an old man came to him and told him about the benefits of the Satyanarayan Puja. The Brahmin thought about performing it, but did not act upon his intention. When he finally did so, he became rich. Then a woodcutter passed by and learned about this ceremony and began to perform it regularly as well. He too became wealthy.

The second story is about a merchant who was childless. One day he came upon a wise and pious king and asked him what he was doing. The king replied that he was performing a katha so Lord Satyanarayan would fulfill his wish for a son. The merchant went home and told his wife, Leelavati, about the katha and both agreed to perform it once they had a child. Ten months later, Leelavati gave birth to a beautiful daughter whom they decided to name Kalavati. Leelavati kept reminding her husband about their promise but the merchant said they would fulfill it at the time of Kalavati's wedding. Kalavati became a beautiful young woman and she was married to fine young man.

Unfortunately, the merchant forgot all about the puja. A few days after the marriage, the merchant set off with his son-in-law for business. The two arrived at a village where they anchored their boat. Just at that time, thieves, who had robbed a king and were fleeing from the king's guards, left their loot in the merchant's boat. The guards found it and accused the merchant and his son-in-law of the theft. As a result, the two men were imprisoned. Meanwhile, Leelavati and Kalavati were robbed of all their wealth and had to beg for food. One day, Kalavati passed a home where a Satyanarayan Katha was in progress. After stopping to listen and partaking of the *prasad*, blessed food, that was passed around, she returned home and told her mother what she had heard. Leelavati and Kalavati immediately made preparations to perform the puja. Shortly thereafter, the king who had imprisoned the merchant and his son-in-law dreamed that the two men were innocent and had them released with their wealth restored.

The third story continues the story of the merchant. While he was on his way home, Lord Satyanarayan, disguised as an old man, approached him and asked him what he had in his boat. The merchant replied that he had only leaves and hay. A few minutes later, the merchant felt his boat lighten. When he checked, he saw that his cargo had indeed turned into leaves and hay. He sought out the old man whom he understood to be God and apologized for his lies, promising to worship God faithfully. When he and his son-in-law returned home, Leelavati and Kalavati were in the midst of the katha. Without finishing and without taking the blessed food, Kalavati rushed off to greet her husband. Lord Satyanarayan caused the boat to disappear and Kalavati to faint. Shocked, the merchant again begged God for forgiveness. God told him that Kalavati would be able to see her husband once she completed the katha and respectfully took the prasad. Kalavati heard God's voice and hurriedly returned to finish the ceremony and have the blessed food. When she went back to meet her husband, she found him well and content. The grateful family lived happily and comfortably and continued to form this puja regularly thereafter.

The final story is about a king who, though generous toward his subjects, showed disrespect to Lord Satyanarayan. One day when he was hunting in a forest, he came upon a few villagers who were performing the Satyanarayan Puja. The villagers offered the king prasad, but the king did not accept it. When he returned to his kingdom, he found everything destroyed and his one hundred sons lying dead on the floor. He understood that this was the result of his arrogant refusal of the prasad. He returned to the forest, joined in the ceremony, and partook of the blessed food, which was nectar consisting of milk, curds, sugar, ghee (clarified butter) and honey. The king took some nectar back home and put a little in the mouths of each of his sons. They all came back to life and lived happily, performing the Satyanarayan Katha faithfully thereafter.

After the fourth story is finished, we are told that the Brahmin, the merchant and the king all enjoy happy future incarnations and attain salvation. We are also reminded that all those who faithfully perform this ritual will be similarly freed from suffering, that their wishes will be fulfilled and that they will be released from the cycle of birth and death. The priest who conducted the ceremony blesses the participants on whose wrists he has tied a cotton string dyed in the red powder known as sindoor or *kanku*. Traditionally, the sanctified string is left on until it falls off from wear. It is then preserved or respectfully discarded in flowing water.

Like all pujas, this one in honor of Lord Satyanarayan concludes with the circulation of a tray containing the sacred flame of knowledge accompanied by clapping, by ringing of cymbals and bells, and by singing of praises to God. One by one, all the attendees are invited to put their hands above the fire and then on their eyes and all are invited to commune with God by partaking of the sweets and fruit that have been offered to Him and that He has blessed.

Although the stories that are told as part of the katha are simple, though perhaps somewhat extreme, they make a point and their symbolism is clear. God in the guise of an old man fits the image of divine wisdom that people may create in their minds. God's appearance itself can be imagined or real. Participation in the ceremony often leaves a feeling that there may be some value in listening to the tales. Tales abound of wishes that became fulfilled as soon as someone pledged to perform this ceremony. Moreover, the idea that the Absolute Spirit speaks to us in visions or dreams is natural to those who believe in a supreme being. The katha also illustrates the workings of karma. Because the stories are familiar to most listeners, their minds are free to wander through the telling so worshippers can speculate about their own lives and wishes and consider the value of honoring their own promises.

Rituals surrounding death are the last ceremonies that Hindus experience. These rites of transition are intended not only to bring peace to the mourners, but also to assist the passage of the soul into the next plane. Hinduism maintains that we are active participants in our own death. Death is a process that we can prepare for throughout our life and particularly in the moments before our death. Old people who are blessed have been known to predict their time of death and people who are ill can delay their death until they see and bless their loved ones. It is said that the thoughts of a dying person may to an extent determine what his or her future incarnation will be.

At death, the soul sheds its body and passes through heavenly or hellish realms that exist simultaneously in consciousness and in the universe that is its reflection. When they die, those who lack in faith and goodness are destined to pass through the lower regions of misery, anger, and fear on the way to rebirth in inferior bodies. The virtuous come to dwell in the upper heavenly regions of happiness before becoming reborn as pure, noble beings. The recital of mantras around a departing or departed soul is believed to improve the soul's karma, to ease its passage from earthly to astral regions, and to assist it in detaching from its physical body.

Cremation or incineration is the only way that practicing Hindus dispose of the dead. Whenever possible, the eldest son lights the fire that will burn the body or else pulls the switch that will start the incineration. Cremation finalizes the freeing of the soul and returns the body to earth, fire, water, air and ethereal atmosphere, the five elements of which it is made. After cremation the ashes are scattered in the holy Ganga River, if possible, or else into the ocean or another river or a body of water. Traditionally cremation takes place as soon as possible after death.

The manner in which families observe funeral rites pertaining to preparation of the body, to the performance of ceremonies, and to the specifics of the rites themselves varies considerably in different communities and in different parts of India. However, two customs prevail. The first is an occasion for the family of the deceased to receive respects and condolences from friends and acquaintances. Within a few days of the funeral, almost all Hindus announce a time and place for people to come and acknowledge both the life of the deceased and the loss suffered by the bereaved. This gathering is a silent seating. It is a time for all who have a connection with the deceased or his family to visit. People arrive always wearing white clothes. Not a word is said. Nods, tears, and waves are the most that may be exchanged. After sitting in silence for a while, the visitors depart understanding that their quiet presence counted a great deal.

The second custom honors the life of the deceased and enables his or her loved ones to become once again occupied with the business of life. Generally on the fourteenth day after the death of someone who had a long life, the immediate family of the deceased hosts a memorial dinner. This dinner should be a happy occasion that marks the beginning of remembrance and helps to soften the pain and to fill the emptiness in the hearts of those who must carry on. It is the first of many celebratory dinners that these families will come to enjoy in honor of their new ancestor.

Beyond celebration of life landmarks, the Hindu calendar marks the passing of weeks, of fortnights, of months, of seasons, and of years with holidays and festivals. Hindus worship and celebrate days that are sacred to different deities. They eat only milk, fruits, and nuts on certain days of the week and on days that the moon cannot be seen. They celebrate many full moons and the whole extra month that comes around every third year to reconcile the lunar and solar calendars. Girls love and honor their brothers and adopted brothers on special days and perform elaborate rituals to get a good husband and to bring prosperity and well-being to the husbands they already have. Not everyone celebrates everything, but certain major holidays cannot be missed.

On January 14th, Hindus mark the beginning of Uttarayan, the sun's journey to the north. This is the only Hindu festival that follows the solar calendar. In some parts of India, Uttarayan is celebrated by a huge kite flying festival. The city of Ahmedabad in Gujarat is famous on this day for its sky filled with colored kites, with only corners of blue peeking out behind them. Aficionados prepare for this occasion for weeks, choosing kites, choosing string, and testing the powdered glass that they apply to the string so as to cut kites flown by others. Strings already glazed with glass are an option, but pros have their own formula. Young people learn from their elders what kites fly best, what the thickness of the string ought to be, how best to tie tails on the kites, and how finely glass should be crushed. Test matches go on for days, and finally the big day comes and the whole city climbs to rooftops. In recent years, certain fields and sites are also set aside for kite flying during Uttarayan. Children chase fallen kites as far as they can run. At dusk, persistent flyers attach lanterns to their kites. Into the night, tallies are made and people finally wind down. Kite flying continues on January 15th, but this day is tinged by tiredness, by fingers that are bleeding in spite of the leather shields that were worn, and by a bit of disappointment because Uttarayan is soon going to be over.

The spring festival, Holi, is a fun filled event enjoyed all over India. It is celebrated sometime around March. The name Holi comes from Holika Dhahan, which means the burning of the Demoness Holika. This festival symbolizes the triumph of good over evil. Effigies of various demons are burned in bonfires. Throughout India on Holi crowds take to the streets to participate in splashing buckets of bright colored water or spraying colored powder on their friends and passersby. Those who do want to be splashed or sprayed are best off staying home.

Lord Rama, Lord Krishna, and Ganesh are worshipped on their legendary birthdays. In March or April devotees of Lord Rama recite the *Ramayana* in His honor. In July or August, Lord Krishna's worshipers fast until midnight when a reenactment of His divine birth takes place followed by a day of festivity and ceremony. People celebrate Ganesh's birthday by carrying his image, garlanded and adorned, through the streets. They sing and dance in a spirit of love and merriment. Lord Shiva's devotees worship Him on His great night known as Maha Shivratri. Those who worship the female energy of the Mother Goddess celebrate her forms as Durga and as Kali in autumn. In some parts of India, Durga Puja is the considered the most important holiday of the year, outshining even the Festival of Lights.

For the majority of Hindus, Diwali or Deepavali, the Festival of Lights, is the most meaningful and most enjoyable religious celebration of the year. Several weeks before, shops stock up. Streets and homes light up. The Hindu community makes new purchases, refurbishes its homes and wardrobes, and otherwise gets ready to pray and to party. About a month before the Festival of Lights, Indians celebrate Navratri, the Nine Night Festival. The Gujarati community of Western India performs particularly colorful folk dances. For some or all of nine nights, women and some men gather dressed in the traditional attire of their state. The dance is called *garba* and it is performed in a circle with wooden sticks that women and men beat together to mark the rhythm of their steps.

Deepavali means a row of lights. Traditionally people make lights or lamps by lighting *diyas*, cotton wicks soaked in oil that are placed in little clay pots. The flames are made in the same way as the flames made for pujas. They are arranged in trays scented with camphor. Today, the diyas are often supplemented by candles, bulbs, and all manner of lighting. The purpose of the Diwali lamps is to light the path of Lakshmi, the Goddess of Wealth and Prosperity, so she is certain to visit and bless her worshippers and their homes. At the same time, the Diwali flames symbolize inner illumination.

Diwali is celebrated on the fourteenth day of the lunar month Kartika which comes in October or November. It is the day of the dark moon that cannot be seen. The next day, when the new moon of the month Aswin appears, the New Year begins. The day of the dark moon also commemorates the return of Lord Rama from exile and the killing of the demon, Narakasura. However, Diwali is essentially a year end and a New Year celebration.

A few days before Diwali, people decorate their homes with new or fresh furnishings and with flowers and leaves. The most talented family members make a big colorful design called a *rangoli* at the entrance, using grains and rice or paints. Sweets are prepared for guests who will come to call. Generally, a day before Diwali, known as the thirteenth day of prosperity, Hindus ask Lakshmi, who brings wealth and good fortune, to bless their account books so that their businesses and finances may flourish.

On or around Diwali most families hold a puja in their homes to pay their respects to God, to Lakshmi and to their elders. These days of festivity often include a visit to the nearest temple or shrine. At dusk all the lights in homes and businesses are turned on. Fireworks are lit. People give parties, visit one another, and gather to play cards.

For three or four days of festivity and worship, Hindus dress up in their finery and jewelry. They call on friends and receive envelopes with gifts of money from employers and elders. They exchange greetings with loved ones who are far away. They send gifts of sweets. In India and in other countries with a significant Hindu population, Diwali is a national holiday. It is a big social and cultural event where friends and families meet, enjoy themselves, and celebrate their culture and their heritage.

Observing Diwali or joining in any of the vast array of rituals, traditions, and festivities that complement Hindu philosophy is optional, but friends, families and the collective Hindu mindset make them difficult to ignore. Religious ceremonies contain a component of social and familial obligation. They are fluid rather than highly orchestrated events, but attendance matters. Ceremonies or pujas provide opportunities to meet and greet friends and relatives, even while participants are busy performing rituals. Even the most important ceremonies, like weddings, are not rehearsed. If glitches occur, people improvise. Thus, no one considers an impromptu conversation in the midst of a ceremony out of order.

Except for the silence at funeral gatherings, Hindu ceremonies are a back drop for interaction. Silent observation is not the essence of respect, though occasionally when something of particular importance is said or done or when people become too rowdy, there may be calls for less noise.

Often generic Hindu ceremonies are dedicated to the worship of God in His formless essence. Rituals held around sacrificial fires that do not honor any specific representation of God are known as *havans*. However, figures, symbols, or photographs of God's manifestations are common in most rituals. Many Hindus wonder whether worship centered on imagery or on ritualistic acts even without imagery truly purifies the spirit or promotes kindness or spirituality. Yet such skeptics often find themselves performing or attending pujas and havans. They do so out of respect or to honor a tradition that marked their childhood and remains a part of Hinduism's living memory. Even disbelievers and those who are not really social find themselves engaged in quite a few ceremonies and celebrations.

Skepticism is a hallmark of Hinduism. But it goes hand in hand with a system of beliefs that has been ingrained in Hindu minds for thousands of years, a system that has become their second nature. Thus, the vast majority of Hindus, even those who doubt, step in the footsteps of those who believe the words spoken in the *Bhagavad Gita*:

> A puja is a ceremony for God.
> It is a sacrifice.
> The puja is Brahma.
> The fire which is part of the puja is Brahma.
> Brahma is God's absolute, everlasting power.
> We cannot see or hear or feel Brahma.
> Reaching Brahma and understanding
>     Brahma
> is the reason for the puja.

> (*Gita* 4:24, 25, 26)

## *Chapter Eight*

# Dharma

A person who does everything for God's sake
is free and becomes a part of God.
Doing your duty for God's sake
is the secret.

(*Gita* 23)

**R**ELIGIONS CREATE COMMUNITIES that are united by shared philosophy and belief. These communities in turn develop socio-cultural value systems. As the socio-cultural composition of a community evolves, the religion that gave it birth must adapt itself or reinterpret itself to endure. However, it must do so without surrendering any of its basic beliefs or principles. Otherwise the religion becomes diluted and ceases to be itself.

Hinduism has had a long and vigorous life and throughout it has upheld the Vedic value system known as the Eternal Law, or the Sanatana Dharma.

A value may be a principle, an ideal, a standard, or a priority. It is a lodestar that determines what matters to a person, to a family, and to a community. It determines what choices people make, where they direct their efforts, and how they develop and maintain relationships. A value is not a religious belief, but it reflects the ideas that religious beliefs endorse.

The value system of Hinduism seems to have emerged as a full blown system, already part of the society in which it matured. Early Vedic scriptures contain its seeds, seeds that continue to blossom and bear fruit today. From the onset, Vedic literature has explicitly valued family life and the nurturing of children, hospitality, self-esteem, the pursuit of knowledge, the pursuit of prosperity, the pursuit of happiness, respect for elders and teachers, living in harmony with all beings, avoidance of needless violence and, most importantly, fulfillment of duty. Doing one's duty means following the path of righteousness or living in accordance with the principle of dharma which embraces all other values.

Dharma is a term that does not lend itself to translation. We cannot define dharma in modern languages nor can we pinpoint the time when this term first came about. It belongs to an ancient language that probably pre-dates Sanskrit. The world vision behind the idea of dharma is also ancient. We know that the concept of dharma existed before the birth of Zarathustra, who founded Zoroastrianism, the ancient religion of Persia. Zarathustra is believed to have lived before 1500 BCE. Hinduism and Zoroastrianism have common roots and they both consider dharma, called "daena" in Persian, the path to enlightenment. "Daena" has been translated as religion, righteousness or virtue, social order, revelation, and as eternal law. Daena is essentially dharma.

The term dharma is used to mean "religion" or "the religious way" but these usages do not explain its full meaning. In Buddhism, Dharma refers to the body of Lord Buddha's teaching. In Hinduism, dharma may be best described as a principle by which human beings must abide in order to be good, to be happy, to get positive karma and to become liberated from the material world. The Sanskrit root of the word dharma means to maintain or to sustain, so dharma is the principle that maintains the universe. In the *Gita*, when Lord Krishna says we must do our duty and fulfill our dharma, He means we must play our part in maintaining universal order. Our own dharma is our own individual law:

> People must do things which are their duty whether they feel like doing them or not.
> Your own duty is greater than anyone else's, even if your duty is to die.

(*Gita* 3:35)

Thus, dharma is both a universal principle and a personal principle. Dharma guides the universe, society, and individuals. According to Vedic scripture, it is truth:

> Dharma is truth.
> It is said that
> one who speaks truth
> speaks dharma
> and one who speaks dharma
> speaks truth.
>
> (*Bhridaranyaka Upanishad* 1.4.14)

Dharma is a lodestar not only for Hindus but also for Zoroastrians, Buddhists, Jains, and Sikhs. It is an abiding principle by which the followers of these religions live. Dharma is a sacred duty that must be fulfilled.

Dharma gives every human being a place and a role within which individuals have a chance to improve their position in the world until they are free of its bindings. They have an opportunity to write their own destiny to make things better for themselves and to make a difference in the world. To do so, they have to think about what is good. Hinduism teaches that responsibility, compassion, spirituality, piety, selflessness, and renunciation are good and these ideas have become ideals. Scripture, society, and culture have translated Hindu ideals into values that in turn determine behavior. Hinduism expects its followers to engage in behavior that promotes the greatest good and this entails living by the principle of dharma.

Dharmic principles mandate behavior that relates to family life, social life, and spiritual life. These principles are not exclusive to Hinduism, but they are specifically integral to Hindu thought. Dharmic laws are both natural and learned, passed on from generation to generation.

Teaching children the Sanatana Dharma which is the heart of the Hindu value system has become a challenge in the twenty-first century. As families are separated, as Hindus live more and more in the midst of other communities, as mothers and grandmothers work, and as information overload impinges upon time, it takes more and more of a focused effort to raise children in accordance with traditional values. Customs that passed on from generation to generation naturally now have to be passed on purposefully.

While children used to learn, understand, and practice Hinduism effortlessly, now families must teach them its meaning. In the past, children grew up speaking the languages of their ancestors, languages full of symbolism and meanings that cannot be well expressed in other tongues. Today parents must persevere in teaching children the languages and ways of their elders.

Family life in Hinduism is not limited to husband, wife, and children. Even though joint families are becoming less of a norm, relationships between family members are fine tuned. In Hindu families, the words brother and sister are usually used to refer to cousins. A first cousin is a cousin brother or a cousin sister, distinguished from a sibling who is a real blood brother. Hindus refer to older brothers and sisters and to younger brothers and sisters differently. They use specific words to describe their precise relationship to their brothers and sisters as well as to their aunts and uncles. Separate terms are used to define an elder or a younger brother-in-law or sister-in-law. Indian languages also use different words to refer to an aunt who is their mother's sister, to an aunt who is their father's sister and to aunts who are the spouses of their mother or father's brother. Similarly uncles are distinguished by their exact connection. Different traditions pertain to aunts and uncles who are related in different ways. Only the English words Auntie or Uncle are generic and these are used generally to show respect to elders.

Indian languages also have separate words for grandparents on the mother's side and grandparents on the father's side. Families of North Indian origin call the mother's parents Nana and Nani, Grandpa and Grandma. Their call their father's father Dada and their father's mother Dadi. This terminology reflects the importance of the relationship and the fact that relationships with their two sets of grandparents are different because of tradition.

The *raksha bandhan* ceremony underlines the importance of the special life-long ties that girls have to their brothers and to friends they choose to treat as brothers. Raksha bandhan is a happy ceremony celebrated in July or August. The word *raksha* means protection. On this day, girls tie a colorful thread bracelet called a *rakhi* on their brothers' wrists. By wearing this bracelet, brothers, cousins, and adopted brothers pledge to protect their sisters. They give their sisters gifts and sisters in turn serve their brothers a festive meal. Once a woman ties a rakhi on someone, she considers him her rakhi brother.

Extended familial relationships and friendships among Hindus are demanding and perhaps intrusive, but they offer ongoing satisfaction, encouragement, comfort, and entertainment. In traditional Hindu society, people are expected to extend hospitality not only to family and friends, but also to visitors and even to strangers. Today, it may not be possible or wise to fulfill the obligations of hospitality in the way these obligations were envisioned in the past, but hospitality remains a duty.

The Sanskrit word for guest is *athithi* which means one who has no fixed date or time. This means that a guest may come and go at any time. A well-known phrase from the *Upanishads* says that a guest should be treated like God. Hospitality is the prescribed way to honor one's fellow man and mankind. It is one of the five main religious duties of a householder. The other four duties are honoring God, the *Vedas* and sages, honoring the gods and celestial elements, honoring ancestral spirits and honoring all beings in creation.

Hindu culture requires an overt showing of respect to parents, elders and teachers. It hopes and expects that gestures like bowing to touch their elders' feet will translate into true sentiment and that children will continue to respect their parents through deeper gestures like taking their parents' opinions seriously and caring for them in old age. It is understood that real respect must be earned before it is given. Thus, Hindu values expect parents to consider rearing children their first priority and expect children to honor their parents in return.

Along with elders, Hinduism asks its followers to respect gurus and teachers. Gurus are more than teachers in the sense that their knowledge is believed to be deep and to contain a sacred component. Hindu philosophy has never fully separated secular teachings from spiritual teachings. The pursuit of any knowledge is a sacred pursuit because knowledge cannot exist outside of truth and truth is absolute.

To get knowledge means to learn the truth.
To learn you must bow down with respect
    to the wise.
You must serve them and wait on them
with a pure heart
and they will teach the truth to you.

(*Gita* 4:34)

The pursuit of excellence in a skill is also revered. Excellence in skills like archery can only be attained through spiritual discipline and Hinduism honors gurus who can pass their skills on to their disciples. They have precious knowledge to share. They have talent to inspire their students and strength to discipline them. Because of this, respect for gurus and for their teaching is a deeply rooted value.

Hindus value the pursuit of prosperity and happiness as well as the pursuit of learning. Wealth and well-being are worthy of seeking; poverty is not viewed as a blessing. Rather, it is viewed as penance for past bad deeds. Arrogance, anger, lack of kindness and ignorance are condemned, but the pursuit of wealth and well-being is blessed.

Scriptures teach moderation. They say detachment from the physical, sensual, and emotional world is the way to salvation, but they do not condemn the pursuit or enjoyment of wealth or success. These boons are given to persons who have progressed on the path to enlightenment. Such persons will eventually lose their attraction to the temporal world and will seek God. After many ages , their souls will go to higher planes and thence become liberated and merge into God. Meanwhile, good deeds done in the past will bring prestige, honor, and fulfilled wishes in the present.

*Ahimsa*, or nonviolence, is a Hindu principle that means we should live in harmony with the universe. We should be considerate of all creatures and all natural forces and live in balance with them. We should be compassionate. We should exercise self-control and not go into a frenzy to satisfy our desires, treading on the toes of those who stand in our way. We should be at peace within ourselves and with the world. We should not needlessly hurt others in any way. However, we should do what our duty demands.

While Hinduism, Buddhism, and Jainism all endorse the doctrine of Ahimsa, they consider it differently. Buddhism bans killing along with stealing, lying, sexual misconduct, and intoxication. Jainism opposes all killing categorically. Hindu tenets are not so specific. They go to motive. Hinduism does not oppose killing. Rather, it opposes senseless killing. The distinction is difficult to put into words. The effects of an act depend on the thoughts that engendered it. The doer of the act must decide whether an act is hurtful or not and whether it is necessary or not. It is the quality of the actor's nature that determines if he or she makes the right and good decision and that sets karma in motion, for better or for worse. While a wise person performs acts that are in keeping with universal harmony, an anger driven fool is likely to commit acts of unwarranted violence.

Violence and destruction is not always harmful. Burning fields to improve their fertility is a good thing. It is different from starting a wildfire that will burn and destroy forests. The *Gita* speaks of a moral war, explaining that the soul cannot be killed and that the body does not matter at all. The *Mahabharata* and the *Gita* illustrate rather than explain what constitutes a moral war. Lord Krishna speaks on the "Battlefield of Dharma." The noble hero, Arjun, does not want to slay his enemy. He does not want a kingdom, or victory, or pleasures. He would rather his enemy kill him than kill them. Lord Krishna convinces Arjun to fight, leaving the outcome of the war in God's hands:

> Do not care if your fighting brings pleasure
>     or pain,
> victory or defeat.
> Just do your duty.
> In this way you will be free.

(*Gita* 2:38)

These lines make it clear that Ahimsa, or nonviolence, is not strictly a pacifist doctrine. It may not even be a doctrine as much as an awareness, a consciousness of what human beings need to do to maintain universal harmony and balance.

Similarly, self-esteem is a significant value in Hinduism without being part of any doctrine. Self-esteem is a state of mind. It is an implicit rather than an explicit value in philosophy and culture. Self-esteem is fostered rather than taught. Like nonviolence, it is part of the belief system that upholds the need for human beings to respect one another and to respect universal principles. Reciprocal esteem reflects the honor we give to the whole of creation and that we expect creation to give us.

The deepest reason that Hinduism places importance on self-esteem is its belief that the flame of illumination shines within each of us, the belief that the universe is part of our consciousness and that God or holiness lives in our soul:

God is knowing and God is knowledge.
God is in your heart.

(*Gita* 13:17)

The Hindu greeting *Namaste* accompanied by the reverential *anjali* recognizes the holiness in all human beings. The word Namaste is translated as, "I bow down to you." In Sanskrit, "to bow" means to bow with reverence and this expression is used in invocations to God. Thus, the true meaning of Namaste is "I bow to God in you." The anjali is the gesture made by placing both palms together in front of the heart while bowing the head. It too is a gesture used in prayer. Sometimes the graceful anjali is made without words being spoken. The anjali and a smile are a beautiful way to say hello or good bye.

The spectrum of values embraced by Hinduism does not define it or even set it apart from other value systems, but it represents Hindu ideals. Some of these values belong to all humanity. Others are shared by Hinduism and its sister religions. Yet others may be specific to the Hindu outlook on life. Not every Hindu shares all the values that are part of Hindu teachings. Nor does every value that Hinduism has taught prevail. Yet most of these values have determined Hindu culture and reflected the Hindu world view for many thousands of years.

Morals and ethics are components of values. If people advocate a particular behavior, like telling the truth or showing respect, that behavior becomes a value. Morals are standards that pertain to individuals whereas ethics embrace rules pertaining to societies or societal groups.

In Hinduism, morals and ethics are important, but they do not apply to behavior in the abstract. They apply to behavior in context, taking into account circumstance and motives. While doing or not doing certain things like telling the truth, helping the needy, and not killing are generally the right thing to do, they may not be the right thing to do at all times or in all places or under all circumstances. Thus, rather than taking a stand about matters like telling the truth or killing and then carving out exceptions, Hinduism stays away from making rules cast in concrete, particularly about what we should NOT do. It does not say "Thou shalt not kill" or "Thou shalt not lie" and then carve out exceptions for self-defense or saving a life or sparing someone's feelings. Rather, Hindu scriptures direct people to follow the path of goodness which requires them to be worshipful, to take actions that are in harmony with the universe and humankind, and to pursue true knowledge.

Virtue is its own rule and following dharma, the eternal law, is the highest virtue.

# Chapter Nine

# Truth

Then the Lord said:
Listen to the words *Om Tat Sat.*
These are holy words.
Om means God.
Tat means everything in the world is God.
Sat means truth and goodness.
Those who want to reach God say Om Tat Sat.
These three words explain God.

(*Gita* 17:23, 24, 25, 26)

THE SACRED SYLLABLE Om or Aum is a powerful focal point in meditation and the phrase "Om Tat Sat" is probably the most significant phrase in Hindu philosophy. These three short words encapsulate the totality of Hindu belief.

Om is the infinite, absolute spirit of God and Truth. This word, spoken aloud or in silence, evokes the highest possible energy that goes beyond existence or nonexistence. When chanted, the mantra

Om resonates in the inner world of consciousness and vibrates, echoing through the physical world of perception. In meditation it has the power to take us inward toward the deep clarity of our soul.

Tat means simply "that." However, in relationship with God, the word "that" takes on a greater meaning. It reaffirms Om. Tat means, "God is God, the absolute spirit, and the ultimate truth." Tat also can mean "God is everything" and "Everything comes from God."

"Sat" means true or real. The single word Sat says, "What is true is real and what is real is true." Hindu scriptures describe God, the Absolute Spirit, as the only reality and the only Truth. All else is illusion. All that is not God is not permanent and therefore it is unreal and false. It is Asat, not Truth.

Sat also means virtuous or good when it pertains to people, to actions, or to ideas in the finite physical world. In this world, Sat describes all that is pure, illuminating, and uplifting whereas "Asat," which means not Sat, describes all that is impure, dark, and deluding.

"Om Tat Sat" has been translated and explained in a number of different ways, almost all of which are right because of the many possibilities this combination of concepts contains. The simple complexity of the phrase "Om Tat Sat" expresses a powerful idea. Om in and of itself acknowledges God as the total reality. Added to Om, Tat affirms God as "That that is." Sat concludes that Om is that state of being which is true and real. Thus, the mantra, "Om Tat Sat," glorifies Om as the totality of Truth, saying Om is the only true existence or the only existence that is real. The three words "Om Tat Sat" together can be translated as "God Is True" as well as "God is the Absolute Truth," "All truth is God," "God is the only Truth," "God is That that is True," "God is eternal existence," "God is Reality" and the cumulative sum of all these statements.

Sanskrit vocabulary and syntax enable Hindu philosophy to express elaborate ideas in just a few concentrated words. It is hard to imagine that this philosophy could flourish without the logically brilliant language that gave it expression.

Sat is one of the strongest words in Sanskrit and in Hinduism. Chants, prayers, and teachings use it over and over again, to speak of God, truth, reality, purity, light, and virtue. Sat is the first component of the term "*Satchitananda*," which is the glorious state of liberation and oneness with God. Hinduism considers the attainment of enlightenment, which leads to Satchitananda, the ultimate objective of life. Sat, Chit, and Anand are three ideas joined together to form one comprehensive concept. Sat in Satchitananda is eternal reality. Chit is existence, consciousness, or self-knowledge. Anand is extreme happiness or bliss. Satchitananda describes the three qualities of Brahma, the formless God who is real, who is all knowing, and who is pure ecstasy. The qualities of reality, knowledge and ecstasy reveal themselves to the enlightened soul that has become freed from the bonds of the material world. The soul that experiences Satchitananda becomes a part of the splendor and magnificence of the formless, endless, unfathomable God named Brahma.

The idea of Sat meaning purity reflective of God is central to Hindu Philosophy. Purity is also the best quality of nature and of human nature in comparison with the inferior physical quality characterized as passion and with the lowest quality characterized as ignorant inertia or inactivity. As a human trait, Sat is virtue.

Virtue is filled with truth and goodness, divine qualities that bring us nearer to God. It is opposed to sin which is filled with untruthfulness and evil, demonic traits that distance us from God:

> Goodness leads to God and freedom
> Evil takes you away from God
>
> (*Gita* 16:5)

Those who are *evil* are ignorant. They are tainted by the absence of truthfulness, by lack of virtue and by impurity:

People who are evil
do not know what is right or wrong
So they cannot be pure, or behave well or be
truthful.

(*Gita* 16:7)

The *Bhagavad Gita* explains that sin arises from greed, from unrestrained desire and from the anger that we feel when these desires are not satisfied. Desire causes sin and prevents us from seeing the truth that is God.

Desire covers the truth like dust covers a
mirror
or like smoke covers fire.
Control yourself,
stop desire
and you will see the truth
and you will not sin.

(*Gita* 3:38, 39)

In the view of Hinduism, sinfulness and goodness are mixed in our characters. Our natures contain different proportions of these qualities or tendencies and we should strive to behave in a manner that develops good tendencies and wipes out bad ones. While our deeds reflect our nature, they also impact it. For example, being truthful and worshipping God with a loving heart are signs of persons who are good and doing these things leads to goodness. Conversely, being dishonest or pretending to worship God with a hate filled heart are signs of a person who is evil and doing these things leads to evil.

In chapter sixteen of the *Bhagavad Gita* which discusses goodness and evil, Lord Krishna sums up the tendencies and behaviors that constitute goodness:

> The Lord said:
> Goodness is many things.
> Goodness is being brave and pure
> and thinking of your soul.
> Your soul is God inside you.
> Goodness is helping others.
> It is self-control and worshipping God
> and having pujas
> and studying the *Vedas* and other holy
>     books.
> It is calling out God's names and glories
> and suffering for your beliefs.
> Goodness is being straight and strong
> in body and mind.
> Peacefulness, truthfulness, and kindness
>     are good.
> Goodness is realizing God does things
>     through you,
> that you do not do them by yourself.
> Goodness is not wanting,
> being kind to all
> and not caring about the pleasures of your
>     body.

> Goodness is gentleness
> and being ashamed of your mistakes
> and not being lazy.
> Forgiveness, strength
> not being mean and not being proud
> are goodness.
> These are the signs of someone who is good.

(*Gita* 16:1, 2, 3)

This passage shows that goodness is not tied to any particular code of conduct nor does it arise from obeying a particular set of rules. There are no clear cut rules a person can follow to become good. Rather, acting virtuously cultivates goodness and the state of goodness causes a person to act virtuously. Vedic philosophy views goodness as a state of being that can be achieved through self-conditioning. It is a pursuit that lasts for lifetimes.

People who sincerely aspire to goodness attain goodness. Those who wish to become brave, pure, pious, disciplined, worshipful, knowing, tranquil, truthful, kind, gentle, modest, energetic, forgiving, and strong will become these things and will become good. They will become wise and make good decisions. They will perform noble deeds that will benefit the world. They will find themselves on the path to enlightenment and they will find happiness. They will attain salvation. Hinduism offers no shortcuts to salvation. It offers no single principle that people can embrace to be saved if they are not good. In order to be freed, a person must first become good.

Goodness is wisdom and gentleness, whereas evil is ignorance and arrogance. Those who are good are knowing, whereas those who are bad and do bad things are unknowing. Such people act out of selfishness, unkindness, and hypocrisy. They consider that no power is higher than their own. They seek worldly pleasure at any cost. They have no virtue and no shame. They are deluded:

> These people who do not understand are
> cruel.
> They are born to ruin things
> They are dishonest, proud, rude, and
> foolish.
> Fools keep worrying and worrying.
> They only care about their body.
> They make wrong decisions.
>
> (*Gita* 16:9, 10, 11)

The deluded are impelled by lust, anger, and greed, the three gateways to the lower worlds of hell. They are condemned to rebirth after rebirth in the bodies of fools. But even so, they carry the spark of divine truth within. Although the light of truth flickers in their hearts, wrongdoers cannot see it because confusion covers it up.

Not all can see Me
because their minds
are covered by foolishness and desire.
they are confused by opposites,
like wanting and hating,
and their confusion covers up the truth
which is God.

(*Gita* 7:27)

But if the confusion is dispelled, even the worst
sinners will be transformed. Love of truth will change
their nature and cause goodness to prevail in their
minds and hearts:

Even the worst people, even sinners, are good
if they love me with all their heart.
They become good very quickly
and become happy forever.

(*Gita* 9:30)

In Hindu philosophy, goodness, truth, and God are
one. God is absolute goodness and eternal truth. The
Absolute Soul that is God illuminates the soul of all
beings. However, human goodness is a material human
trait. The human traits of goodness and evil both pertain to the body, not to the spirit. In Hindu thought,
the mind is part of the body. It is the energy that powers our intellect, our judgment, and our ego, but it is
temporal and it is shed when the soul is released from
the bondage of repeated reincarnations. The body and

mind are matter whereas the soul is spirit. A particular life comes into being when the spirit and the body join together and it ends when the soul and the body separate at death.

When it embodies, the soul, the kernel that is our innermost divine spirit, is covered by four layers of being. The soul itself is counted as a fifth layer, though it is pure essence and is devoid of matter. It is the unchanging soul named God. The five layers of being are called *kosas*. The four layers surrounding the soul can be understood to be sheaths, shells, or husks or vessels. The kosas increase in density as they move outward, further away from the spirit. The layers closest to our soul make up our ethereal or astral body whereas the outermost layer is heavy with matter.

The fourth sheath, nearest to the soul, is knowledge. It is the highest level of understanding and sensitivity that is closest to God. The third sheath is the mind. It is intellect and it contains our memory, causes our dreams, and processes the information that we have taken in through our minds and senses. It also manages the collective information we may call human instinct or intuition. This collective information belongs to all mankind. The second sheath is vitality. It is the vital force that moves the body and makes it work. This is the subtle body that controls our senses and actions as well as internal bodily functions like the pumping of the heart. The fourth outermost sheath is the dense physical body itself.

The living body has three attributes or properties called gunas. These attributes are our tendencies or natures. Ranking from highest to lowest, the three gunas are sattva, rajas, and tamas. Sattva is the tendency of the highest and purest of beings. It is true and good. Rajas is the tendency of dynamic beings filled with energetic or frenetic passion. It is not good, but not evil. Tamas is the tendency of ignorant and inert beings. It is bad. People are a mixture of these three traits but our nature depends on which trait is strongest:

> When Sattva is strongest we are wise.
> When Rajas is strongest, we are greedy
> and we cannot keep calm or still.
> When Tamas is strongest,
> we are lazy, foolish, and covered by
> darkness.

(*Gita* 14:11, 12, 13)

Each of these three characteristics bears its own fruit. The fruit of sattva—coming from Sat—is wisdom. The fruit of rajas, which is passion and activity, is greed. The fruit of tamas, which is lethargy and darkness, is ignorance. These fruits are the fruits of karma, the self-determined destiny of every person. The predominant quality of a person's nature at death decides what his or her future incarnation will be.

Hindus believe that the soul dissolves at death. Those whose natures at that time are primarily sattva will rise upwards to be reborn in worlds of the wise and the pure. On the other hand, those whose natures are mostly rajas when they die will be reborn in the world of material attachment. But those whose natures at their death are tamas will sink to be reborn in deluded ignorant bodies.

Even the pure and the wise are subject to the cycle of birth, death, and rebirth until they attain enlightenment. Then, when they see God, they surrender all attachment to the material world because they realize that God is beyond all the qualities of matter. Enlightenment is the understanding that the highest qualities are not real because they spring from the body:

> If you understand
> that God is past Sattva, Rajas, and Tamas,
> Your spirit will be freed from the body.
> It will not have to be born again
> and you will go straight to God.

( *Gita* 14:19, 20)

In addition to describing eternity and virtue, the word Sat is used to explain reality as opposed to illusion. Reality is realization that God alone is real. In this sense Sat is transcendental truth. It is truth that goes beyond human experience but lies within the range of what may be known. Reality is the eternal and unchanging essence of God. All else is Asat, unreality, because it is temporal and changing. The appearance of solidity and permanence that the material universe takes on is an illusion:

> Everyone thinks that the things in the
> world are real,
> but only I, God, am real and unchanging.
> Everything else is make believe.
> Only people who understand God can
> understand this.
> Only the wise can understand that God
> alone is real.
> The world seems real because I use my divine Maya
> to make it appear.
> Maya is make believe. It is magic.
> It causes the world and everything in it
> to seem solid and permanent.
> But the things in the world are always
> moving
> and always changing.
> That is why they are not real
> and they do not last forever.
> Only God is forever real.

> (*Gita* 7:12, 13)

The illusion that the world is real is *Maya*. Maya is a veil that emanates from God's creation. It is the whimsy of matter. Maya covers up truth. It is not the opposite of reality or of unreality. Rather, it is a mask that conceals reality and makes the ever changing world seem permanent. Maya is a barrier people must cross to know the eternal Self that resides within our soul and that is the Universal Soul:

> The wise who understand God pass beyond
> the world.
> They cross over Maya and reach Me.

> (*Gita* 7:14)

Truth is everything in Hinduism. The Sanskrit word Sat encompasses a universe of thought. It includes ideas about infinity, reality, totality, permanence, knowledge, consciousness, magnificence, purity, and more. It is an elevation of the fathomless over the fathomable.

# Chapter Ten

# In Essence

IN ESSENCE HINDUS worship truth, light, and immortality. Each of these words can be and have been construed in countless ways. In one sense they all mean the same thing and embrace the single idea of existence that goes beyond time, space, and substance. The *Vedas* have called this existence God.

One of the most frequently repeated Hindu prayers asks for enlightenment in these few simple and beautiful words:

> May I go from the untruth to truth
> From darkness to light
> From death to immortality
> Om
> Peacefulness Peacefulness Peacefulness
>
> (*Brihadaranyaka Upanishad* 1.3.28)

OM TAT SAT

# Glossary

*Acintya Bheda Abedha:* One of the six sub schools of the Vedanta school of Hindu philosophy which merges the views of other sub schools.

*Advaita:* A sub-school of the Vedanta school of Hindu philosophy which upholds non-dualism, belief that the divine and the individual soul are indistinguishable and inseparable.

*Advaitism:* Non-dualism, the belief that the divine and the individual soul are one.

*Agami Karma:* Karma influenced by previously determined factors.

*Ahimsa:* Nonviolence.

*anjali:* Gesture made with palms joined together and head bowed.

*Antarloka:* The intermediate dimension in the Hindu universal view.

*Aranyakas:* Forest texts, a part of the *Upanishads.*

*Arjun*: Hero of the Mahabharata War to whom Lord Krishna preached the Gita.

*arti*: Wicks lit in ghee which are used in pujas.

*Asat*: Something not true.

*Atharva Veda*: Metaphysical text, the fourth Veda.

*athithi*: Guest.

*Aum*: Alternate spelling for Om.

*Avatar*: Sanskrit word for descent, used to refer to incarnation.

*Ayodhya*: Ancient city believed to be the birthplace of Rama.

*Bhagavad Gita*: The Gita, sacred book of Hinduism.

*Bhagvan*: God.

*Bhim*: Second Pandava brother.

*Bhuloka*: The physical world, the outermost dimension in the Hindu universal view.

*bindi*: A red dot worn by women on the forehead.

*Brahma*: God, the creator of the world.

*Brahmaloka*: The spiritual world, the innermost dimension in the Hindu universal view.

*Brahman*: The concept of God.

*Brahmanas*: The portion of the *Vedas* consisting of commentaries and including the *Aranyakas* and the *Upanishads*.

*Buddha*: Lord Buddha, the ninth avatar, descent/incarnation of Lord Vishnu, worshipped by Buddhists as the Enlightened One.

*chakras*: Wheels or circles representing centers of consciousness in Yoga.

*Darshana*: Orthodox school of Hindu philosophy.

*Deepavali, Diwali*: Hindu festival of lights preceding the New Year.

*Dharma*: A fundamental concept in Hinduism including the idea of duty and righteousness.

*Dhritarashtra*: The blind king, father of the Kauravas.

*diya*: Small flame symbolizing light of knowledge.

*Draupadi*: Wife of the five Pandava brothers.

*Durga*: The Mother Goddess.

*Durga Puja*: Ceremony honoring Durga.

*Duryodhana*: The ruling king, cousin of the Kauravas.

*Dvaitadvaita*: One of the schools of the Vedanta school of Hindu philosophy which upholds both dualism and non-dualism.

*Dvaitism*: Dualism, in Hinduism the belief that the divine and the individual soul are distinct and eternally separated.

*Ganesh, Ganpati*: Widely worshipped and beloved mythological god with elephant head.

*Ganga*: The Ganges River.

*garba*: Folkloric Dance of Gujarat in Western India.

*Gayatri Mantra*: A chant from the Rig Veda.

*Gita*: The sacred book of Hinduism.

*gunas*: Three attributes of the body or of matter or of human nature: sattva, rajas, and tamas.

*Hanuman*: King of the Vanaras, monkey like creatures who helped Lord Rama.

*Hastinapura*: City of the Elephants, Pandava Capital

*Hatha Yoga*: Yoga of the Body.

*havan*: Worshipping around a holy fire.

*Holi*: Spring festival where people spray colors on one another.

*Ishvar*: One of God's names.

*Jatayu*: The eagle who tried to fight Ravana and rescue Sita.

*Kali Yuga*: The current era in Hindu cosmology.

*Kalki*: The anticipated tenth and final avatar, descent/incarnation of Lord Vishnu predicted to deliver the world from evil and darkness.

*kalpa*: An eon in Hindu cosmology.

*Karanaloka*: Another term for Brahmaloka.

*karma*: Action and the fruit of actions.

*Kauravas*: Cousins and enemy of the Pandavas in the Mahabharata War.

*kosas*: Layers of being surrounding the soul.

*Kriyamana Karma*: Karma that is within our control.

*Krishna*: Lord Krishna, the eighth avatar, descent/incarnation of Lord Vishnu.

*kshatriya*: Warrior.

*kundalini*: Centers of energy within persons.

*Kurma*: The second avatar, descent/incarnation of Lord Vishnu in the form of a tortoise.

*lava*: A brief measurement of time.

*Lakshman*: Lord Rama's brother.

*Lakshmi*: Vishnu's consort, the goddess of prosperity.

*Lanka*: Sri Lanka.

*lokas*: Astral planes or worlds.

*Mahabharata*: The Epic describing the Great Mahabharata War.

*Maheshvara*: Name of Lord Shiva.

*mandap*: A covered decorated platform.

*mantra*: A syllable or phrase used in chanting or in meditation.

*Mantra Yoga*: Yoga of chanting.

*Manusmriti*: The *Laws of Manu* which described and prescribed laws of social conduct.

*Matsya*: The first avatar, descent/incarnation of Lord Vishnu in the form of a fish.

*Maya*: Illusion, unreality.

*mendi*: Henna, a natural dye.

*mundan*: Ceremony celebrating a child's first haircut.

*Namaste*: Hindu greeting.

*Naraka*: The netherworld populated by demons.

*Narasimha*: The fourth avatar, descent/incarnation of Lord Vishnu in the form of a man lion.

*Nataraja*: Shiva, Lord of the dance.

*Navratri*: Nine nights celebrated before Diwali.

*Nikul*: Fourth Pandava brother.

*Nyaya*: One of the six Darshanas, or schools of Hindu philosophy.

*nimesha*: The time span equal to the blink of an eye.

*Om*: A holy word symbolizing God and the universe.

*panchamrit*: Five nectars used in religious ceremonies: clarified butter, milk, yogurt, honey, sugar .

*Pandavas*: The sons of King Pandu and victors in the Mahabharata War.

*Panini*: Author of the definitive Sanskrit grammar.

*paramanu*: Briefest unit of time in ancient Hindu scripture as well as an infinitesimal particle.

*Parvati*: Shiva's consort.

*Prajapati*: Lord of Progeny; one of Brahma, the Creator's, names.

*Parashurama*: The sixth avatar, descent/incarnation of Lord Vishnu in the form of a man named Rama with an ax.

*Patanjali*: Author/compiler of yoga sutras and founder of the Yoga school of philosophy.

*Prahlada*: The son of a demon who was made ruler of the earth and underworld by Narasimha.

*Prarabdha Karma*: The portion of karma that bears fruit in the present lifespan.

*prasad*: Blessed food consumed at the end of pujas.

*puja*: A ceremony to worship God.

*Purva Mimamsa*: One of the Darshanas, or schools of Hindu philosophy.

*Raja Yoga*: Yoga of the mind, royal yoga.

*rajas*: One of the three gunas which relates to physical pleasures.

*rakhi*: A symbolic band or bracelet tied by sisters on their brothers' wrists.

*raksha bandhan*: A ceremony where sisters tie a rakhi on their brothers' wrists to pledge protection.

*Rama*: Lord Rama, the seventh descent/incarnation of Lord Vishnu, glorified in the *Ramayana*.

*Ramayana*: The epic glorifying Lord Rama.

*Ravana*: Demon who abducted Sita.

*Rig Veda*: The first Veda consisting of sacred hymns and chants.

*Sahadev*: Fifth and youngest Pandava brother.

*Sama Veda*: The second Veda containing hymns, some honoring the soma plant.

*Samkhya or Sankhya*: One of the six Darshanas, or schools of Hindu philosophy.

*Sanatana Dharma*: The Eternal Law, Hinduism.

*Sanchita Karma*: Accumulated karma yet to bear fruit.

*Sangeet*: A music and dance event.

*Saraswati*: Brahma's consort, the goddess of learning; name of an ancient river.

*Sat*: True or Truth.

*Satchitananda*: The state of liberation and oneness with God.

*sattva*: One of the three gunas which is pure and good.

*Satyanarayan Katha*: A religious ceremony honoring Lord Satyanarayan.

*Satya Yuga*: The earliest age in Hindu cosmology.

*Shaivite*: Follower of Lord Shiva.

*Shaktism*: Worship of God as both male and female force.

*Shiva or Siva*: God, the destroyer of the world.

*Shuddhadvaita*: Pure non-dualistic philosophy viewing God and the spirit as inseparable.

*sindoor*: Red powder.

*Sita*: Lord Rama's consort.

*Sivaloka*: Another word for Brahmaloka.

*smriti*: Vedic texts that are recollections of sages.

*sruti*: Vedic texts that are revelations.

*sunya or shunya*: Zero; nothingness.

*Surpanakha*: A demoness, sister of Ravana.

*tamas*: One of the three gunas which is impure and bad.

*Tantra Yoga*: A form of yoga that incorporates Shaktism.

*Tat*: A reference to God, "That" that is.

*tikka*: A red dot, or bindi, worn by women on their forehead.

*Treta Yuga*: The second era in Hindu cosmology.

*truti*: A minute fraction of a second .

*Upanishads*: Hindu scripture, philosophical and mystical meditations.

*Uttar or Mimamsa*: Precursor to the Vedanta school of Hindu philosophy.

*Vaisheshika*: One of the Darshanas, or orthodox schools of Hindu philosophy.

*Vaishnavite*: Follower of Lord Vishnu.

**Vamana**: The fifth avatar, descent/incarnation of Lord Vishnu, in the form of a dwarf.

**Vanaras**: Monkey-like creatures who fought with Lord Rama to rescue Sita from Ravana.

**Varaha**: The third avatar, descent/incarnation of Lord Vishnu, in the form of a boar.

**Vedanta**: One of the Darshanas, or schools of Hindu philosophy.

**Vedas**: Ancient Hindu holy books.

**vedha**: One hundred trutis.

**Vedic**: Pertaining to the *Vedas*.

**Vinyasa Yoga**: A form of yoga that coordinates breathing with movement.

**Vishnu**: God, the preserver of the world.

**Visishtadvaita**: Qualified non-dualistic philosophy.

**Vyasa**: Author of the Mahabharata.

**Yajur Veda**: The third Veda prescribing the manner in which rituals should be performed.

**yoga**: A term that means a discipline used to refer to specific paths leading to enlightenment; also one of the six Darshanas, or schools of philosophy.

**Yoga Sutras**: Aphorisms mostly referring to meditation.

**yogi**: One who practices and has mastery of yoga.

**yojana**: A distance of 1,918 miles.

**Yudhishtir**: Eldest Pandava brother.

**Yuga**: Age or era.

# Index

## A

# About the Author

Irina Gajjar was born in Bucharest, Romania and grew up in Manhattan, New York.

She graduated *Magna cum Laude* from Mexico City College (now University of the Americas) at the age of seventeen with a Bachelor of Arts degree in Romance Languages. She also earned a Master of Arts degree in Spanish from Bryn Mawr College in Pennsylvania, a PhD in Ancient Indian Studies from Bombay University in Bombay, India and a JD degree from the University of Texas at Austin.

She speaks eight languages, including Gujarati, Chinese, Spanish, Portuguese, Romanian, and French. She also studied Sanskrit in India for ten years.

Author Residence: Chicago, IL. Previous books: *The Gita: A New Translation of Hindu Sacred Scripture.*